MILITARY COSTUME AND ACCOUTREMENTS IN ANCIENT INDIA

Military Costume and Accoutrements in Ancient India

UMA PRASAD THAPLIYAL

MANOHAR
2012

First published 2012

ISBN 978-81-7304-955-2

Published by
Ajay Kumar Jain *for*
Manohar Publishers & Distributors
4753/23 Ansari Road, Daryaganj
New Delhi 110 002

Typeset by
Umesh Chand Nailwal
Delhi 110 092

Printed at
Salasar Imaging Systems
Delhi 110 035

To

My Aunt (Bua)
Priyamvada Naithani

A Repository of All Wisdom

A Spirit Still and Bright with Something
of an Angelic Light

Contents

List of Illustrations 9

Tansliteration 11

Preface 13

1. WARFARE IN ANCIENT INDIA: A SURVEY 17

Early Phase 17; Vedic Age 17; Age of *Mahājanapadas* 20; Foreign Invasions (First Round) 21; Mauryan Conquests 22; Foreign Invasions (Second Round) 24; Gupta Conquests 26; Vākāṭaka Conquests 27; Road to Instability 27; South Indian Wars 28

2. MILITARY COSTUME: DETERMINING FACTORS 32

Climatic Factor 32; Dress Material—Dyeing and Cleaning 36, Spinning and Weaving 37, Art of Sewing 40; Economic Conditions 41; Military Tactics 42; Foreign Influence 43; Social Bindings 43

3. HARAPPAN AGE 47

Military Disposition 47; Costume 48; Weapons and Accoutrements 49

4. VEDIC AGE 52

Dress Items 53; Body Armour 53; Helmet 55; Brace 55; Weapons 55; Accoutrements 56; *Dhvaja* 58; *Vrātya* Costume 58; Military Vehicles—Chariot and Horse 59

5. SOLDIER IN THE EPICS 65

Concept of Uniform 65; Costume and Accoutrements 66; *Śaṅkha* and *Dhvaja* 70; Long

Hair 70; Body Armour 71; Helmet, etc. 73; Shield 74; Weapons 74; Vehicles of War—Chariot 76, Elephant 78, Horse 80

6. MAURYA-ŚUṄGA AGE 90

Pre-Mauryan Costume 90; Greek Evidence 90; Weapons and Equipment 92; State's Responsibility 93; *Āyudhāgārādhyakṣa* (Superintendent of Armoury) 94; *Sūtrādhyakṣa* (Superintendent of Yarns) 95; Armour (*Kavaca*) 95; Shield (*Carman*) 96; Sword (*Asi*) 97; Bow (*Dhanuṣ*) 99; Sculptural Evidence—Headdress (*Śirovastra*) 101, Garments (*Vastra*) 101, Waist-band (*Kaṭibandha*) 101, Shoes (*Upānaha*) 103, Coiffeur (*Keśavinyāsa*) 103; Vehicles of War—Chariot (*Ratha*) 103, Elephant (*Hastin*) 105, Horse (*Aśva*) 106, Bit (*Khalina*) 107, Girth (*Kakṣya*) 109

7. ŚAKA-KUṢĀṆA AGE 114

Foreign Impact 114; Bhārhut Soldier 117; Sāñcī Portrayals 119; Kilt and Tunic 120; Cross-belts 120; Trousers 120; Fillet 121; Top Boots 121; Armour 122; Helmet 123; Bow 123; Arrow-heads 124; Sword 125; Javelin 126; Shield 126; Mounted Archer 126; Accoutrements of Horse 127; Decline of Chariot 128

8. GUPTA AGE AND AFTER 133

Synthesis 133; Evidence of Bāṇa Bhaṭṭa 134; Headdress 136; Upper Garment 138; Lower Garment 139; Waist-band 141; Footwear 141; Apron (*Ācchādanaka*) 142; Armour 142; Weapons—Bow 143, Sword 143, Shield 144; Vehicles of War—Elephant 144, Horse 145; Purāṇic view 147

Bibliography 153

Index 161

Illustrations

PLATES

1. Harappan soldier after page 48
2. Vedic soldier after page 56
3. Epic soldier after page 72
4. Maurya soldier after page 96
5. Kuṣāṇa soldier after page 120
6. Gupta soldier after page 136
7. Post-Gupta soldier after page 144

FIGURES

1. Statue (Warrior?), Mohenjo-daro 39
2. Soldiers carrying standards (Indus seal) 50
3. Warrior, Bhārhut 98
4. Soldiers in action, Sāñcī 100
5. Archers, Sāñcī 102
6. Chariot, Sāñcī 104
7. Caparisoned elephants, Sāñcī 106
8. Caparisoned horses, Sāñcī 108
9. Mounted standard-bearer, Bhārhut 108
10. Armed warriors, Gandhāra 116
11. Kaniṣka in battle-dress 118
12. Gupta king in military costume 135
13. Elephants on the march, Ajantā 137
14. Army on the march, Ajantā 138
15. Soldiers in action, Ajantā 140
16. Chariot warriors, Ahicchatra 148

Transliteration

अ	a	घ्	gh	प्	p
आ	ā	ङ्	ṅ	फ्	ph
इ	i	च्	c	ब्	b
ई	ī	छ्	ch	भ्	bh
उ	u	ज	j	म्	m
ऊ	ū	झ्	jh	य्	y
ऋ	ṛ	ञ्	ñ	र्	r
लृ	lṛ	ट्	ṭ	ल्	l
ए	e	ठ्	ṭh	व्	v
ऐ	ei	ड्	ḍ	श्	ś
ओ	o	ढ्	ḍh	ष	ṣ
औ	au	ण्	ṇ	स्	s
अँ	m/ṅ	त्	t	ह्	h
अः	h	थ्	th	क्ष्	kṣ
क्	k	द्	d	त्र्	tr
ख्	kh	ध्	dh	ज्ञ	jñ
ग्	g	न्	n		

Preface

In the year 1965, the Ministry of Defence organized a unique display of military costumes of India through the ages at the Republic Day parade. The pageant was repeated during many more parades. I was associated with the preparation of these costumes as a junior officer, and have since been nursing a desire to research the subject more extensively.

The subject is full of constraints as the information available in art and literature is sketchy. The archeological discoveries of Mohenjo-daro and Harappa throw little light on the costume of the people. The *Ṛgveda* which carries graphic descriptions of war, has little to say on the dress of the soldiers. Even the *Mahābhārata* gives no precise information on the costume.

There are conflicting views on many issues related to the subject. It is not known precisely as to when the art of sewing and the use of armour, shoes, coats and trousers started in India. However, by piecing together the scanty information, scattered in art and literature, it is possible to recreate a fairly accurate picture of the Indian soldier's dress in various periods of history.

It is noteworthy that in respect of costume the Indian soldier matched poorly with his Iranian, Macedonian and Central Asian counterparts. *Uṣṇīṣa, uttarīya* and *adhovāsa,* the basic Indian costume, provided him with little protection and mobility. This could well be one of the reasons for his poor performance in the battlefield. His antiquated weapon system was another weakness.

This volume illustrates the costume of soldiers in seven important epochs of Indian history in coloured drawings, based on archaeological, numismatic and literary sources. In some cases, where the source material thus available is inconclusive, informed historical indications have been relied upon. Still, the reader may consider these illustrations as hypothetical creations.

It is remarkable that due to climatic variations, the uniformity of dress was not possible in the country. Further, there were hundreds of kingdoms spread all over India and no uniform dress code could be imposed on them by the central authority, if any. The military tactics and individual preferences may also have influenced the choice of dress among soldiers. This seems to explain the presence of soldiers in different dress styles side by side in the art of Sāñcī, Gandhāra and Ajantā. The foreign invaders added to this variety substantially.

This study is a humble effort to unravel a little known aspect of Indian history. It is hoped that it would attract the attention of scholars in a greater measure and lead to more extensive studies in the military history of India.

I am grateful to the Indian Council of Historical Research for granting me Senior Fellowship to conduct research on a subject so dear to me. I am also grateful to Dr. S.N. Prasad and Dr. B.N. Sharma, my seniors in the Historical Section, Ministry of Defence, Dr. Romila Thapar, my teacher and Shri L.M. Thapliyal, my cousin, for their guidance. My brothers Shri S.P. 'Suman' Thapliyal and Late Shri B.P. Thapliyal and my wife Sarojini have always been a source of inspiration to me. My thanks are also due to my friends Sarvashri, R.S. Bisht, G.B. Singh, D.D. Nautiyal, H.N. Nautiyal, Jaswinder Singh, Umesh Chand Nailwal, Dr. (Smt.) Rewa Dhanedhar and Smt. Karuna Srivastava who have helped me in various measures to complete this work. The Directorate General, Archaeological Survey of India, the National Museum, New Delhi, and the Rampur Raza Library, Rampur kindly supplied me with necessary photographs. In the end I express my gratitude to my brother Late Shri Dwarika Prasad Thapliyal who gave me the vision to see the world of letters.

I am also grateful to M/s Manohar Publishers & Distributors, who gladly agreed to publish this book.

The book is dedicated to the sacred memory of my aunt (Bua) Priyamvada Naithani, a child widow, whom I have always adored as a mother.

UMA PRASAD THAPLIYAL

CHAPTER 1

Warfare in Ancient India: A Survey

EARLY PHASE

The earliest evidence of organized warfare in India is met among the Indus valley people. They appear to have maintained armies. Their cities were encircled by forts, against external threat. They used weapons like mace, axe, dagger, bow, sling, etc. to ward off attack. Defensive weapons such as shield, helmet and armour may also have been known to them.

The military aspect of the Indus Valley civilization has been summed up by Irfan Habib as follows:

> An 'Indus empire' could thus have been created for this to happen. However, the original Indus state needed to have the armed means to both conquer and keep in subjection a large population. There is evidence for fighting with spears (figure 2.23) and for bow and arrow (figure 2.24) from seals; and axe blades in copper or bronze have been found in some profusion.... Nor should the light ox-cart be overlooked. A precursor of the horse-drawn chariot, it could give mobility; and a charge of ox-chariots could dispense resisting infantry. Finally, the walls of the Indus cities and citadels provided sufficient protection against possible surprise attacks by primitive opponents. It is difficult to support the view, in the force of this evidence, that the Indus state did not have sufficient military power to maintain itself.[1]

VEDIC AGE

It is believed that the Indus Valley civilization was followed by Vedic civilization around 1500 BC. While marching from Sindh to Bengal the Āryans may have fought many battles with the natives, whom they called Dasyu or Dāsa.[2] Divodāsa, the leader of the Tṛtsu tribe, defeated Sambara, the chief of the Dāsas, in a war.[3] A Puru king even assumed the title *trasadasyu* after his conquest of Dasyus.[4]

The *Ṛgveda* also refers to some battles fought between various Āryan tribes.[5] Divodāsa, the Tṛtsu king, fought many battles or skirmishes with Turvaśas, Yadus, Purus[6] and some other tribes.[7] In a fierce battle on the banks of the Paruṣṇī (Rāvī), Sudās is said to have defeated a confederacy of ten kings.[8] Among the defeated kings, two were drowned and one died fighting. Sudās also defeated a confederacy of Ajas, Śigru and Yakṣu tribes led by Bheda, a non-Āryan king.[9]

The battles continued during the later Vedic period (1000-500 BC). The Brāhmaṇa literature refers to some battles fought between the Asuras and Devas.[10] The battle fought between Bharata Dauhṣanti and Sātvatas on the bank of Gaṅgā, which ended in the defeat of the latter, was particularly ferocious.[11] Another battle was fought between Śatānīka, Satrājita and Dhṛtarāṣṭra, in which the former emerged victorious.[12]

This was also the time when Āryan civilization was spreading towards the east and the south. It could not have been a peaceful affair. In the process many old Āryan tribes faded out and some new ones emerged. The famous Bharata tribe was replaced by Kuru-Pañcālas and tribes like Anu, Druhyu and Turvaśa lost their pre-eminence. Rituals like *Aśvamedha, Vājapeya* and *Rājasūya* came into vogue as a manifestation of the military might.[13] The Vedic tribal chiefs now came to be called *Adhirāja, Rājādhirāja, Samrāṭ, Virāṭ* and *Ekarāṭ*,[14] depending on the military prowess exercised by them.

In the great epics there are numerous references to wars. The Pāṇḍavas subjugated a large number of kingdoms as a prelude to their *Rājasūya-yajña.*[15] In the Kurukṣetra war, almost all kingdoms of India participated, siding either with the Kauravas or the Pāṇḍavas. Subsequently, Ābhīras destroyed the Vṛṣṇis of Dvārkā.[16] In the war of Laṅkā, the whole family of Rāvaṇa perished.[17] The wars described in the epics could perhaps be related to the later Vedic age.

Frequency of wars in the post-Vedic period is suggested by the discovery of weapons. The Indus Valley people used copper and bronze weapons. Then followed the copper weapons yielded by the copper hoards of Gaṅgā Valley. There is a view that these weapons were manufactured by the Vedic Āryans between 1200 and 1000 BC.[18] Piggot, however, ascribed the authorship of these weapons to the people of Punjab and Indus Valley who came to settle here after the break-up of the Harappan empire.[19] The weapons discovered from the copper hoards include celts, harpoons, antennae swords, spearheads, axes, etc.

But much more important was the use of iron for weapons around 800 BC. The systematic use of iron gradually led to improvement in the quality of weapons.[20] Iron implements and weapons have been found at excavated sites at Atrañjikherā and Jakhera in western UP and adjoining regions which date in the time bracket of the later Vedic period. South Indian megalithic tombs have also yielded a large number of iron weapons. Significantly, the number of iron weapons discoverd here is more than that of agricultural tools and implements.[21]

Evidently, iron was more widely used for weapons than other purposes in early India. This might have added a new dimension to the system of warfare as iron weapons were more solid and lethal than bronze and copper weapons. This might have also necessitated readjustment in the existing strategy and tactics of war.

AGE OF *MAHĀJANAPADAS*

Around 600 BC a new set of soldiers appears on the Indian battlefield. The early Buddhist literature refers to 16 *mahājanapadas*, which included Kāśī, Kośala, Aṅga, Magadha, Vajji, Malla, Cedi, Vatsa, Kuru, Pañcāla, Matsya, Śūrasena, Aśmaka, Avanti, Gandhāra and Kamboja.[22] It also mentions ten republics which included Śākyas of Kapilavastu, Bhaggas of Sumsumagiri, Bulis of Allakappa, Kālamas of Kesaputta, Koliyas of Rāmagāma, Mallas of Pāvā, Mallas of Kuśinārā, Moriyas of Pipphalivana, Videhas of Mithilā and Licchavis of Vaiśālī.[23] The wars fought by these republics and kingdoms are not well recorded but in all probability the rise of four great kingdoms of Magadha, Kośala, Avantī and Matsya on their ruins may not have been a peaceful affair.

The battles fought by the rulers of Magadha, however, find mention in the literature. Bimbisāra (543-492 BC), the earliest known ruler of the kingdom, defeated Aṅgas and subjugated them. His son Ajātaśatru (492-460 BC) defeated the ruler of Kāśī and destroyed the Licchavis after a long drawn war. Subsequently, Śiśunāga, an usurper to the Magadha throne, defeated Pradyota of Avantī and incorporated Madhyadeśa and Mālavā in his empire.[24]

Military activity accelerated during the rule of the Nandas (344-324 BC). The army of Mahāpadma Nanda which comprised 200,000 infantry, 2,000 cavalary, 2,000 four-horsed chariots and 3,000 elephants,[25] vanquished the kingdoms of Ikṣvāku, Kuru, Pañcāla, Kāśī, Śūrasena, Mithilā, Kaliṅga, Aśmaka and Haihaya.[26] It seems that the rulers of Magadha had been able to forge some kind of political unity in eastern India.

FOREIGN INVASIONS (FIRST ROUND)

This was also the time when a number of small states came into existence in north-western and western India. These states maintained large armies but none of them was militarily strong to beat back an invasion. Achaemenid king Cyrus (558-30 BC), taking advantage of the situation, intruded in the Gandhāra region. His successor Darius (522-486 BC) even incorporated Gandhāra and Punjab regions in his empire around 518 BC. Subsequently, the Indians fought alongside the armies of Iran against the Greeks.[27]

Some two hundred years after the first Achaemenid invasion, India was attacked by Alexander, the Macedonian ruler. First he conquered some states of north-west India. But in his battle against Assakenoi (Aśvakas) he had to face a stiff resistance at Massaga fort. Indians fought resolutely and when many of them lay dead or wounded the women picked up their arms to join the battle. Though the Indians lost the battle they 'met a glorious death which they would have disdained to exchange for a life with dishonour'.[28]

Alexander then crossed Indus River near Ohind, subjugated Taxila and Abhisāra and mounted an attack on Poros. Poros joined battle with 50,000 infantry, 3,000 cavalry, 1,000 chariots and 150 elephants. But despite his supremacy in numbers, Poros lost the battle. Alexander then conquered Glaukanikai (Glaucukāyanakas) and occupied their thirty-seven cities. In August 326 BC he crossed the Rāvī and conquered Adraistai (Ariṣṭas) and Kathaians (Kaṭhas). The battle of Sangala against the latter was the bloodiest in which according to Greek sources 17,000 Indians died and 70,000 were imprisoned.

During his homeward journey, Alexander defeated Sophytes (Saubhūti), Siboi (Śivis) and Agalassians

(Agraśreṇīs). The latter while defending their capital inflicted heavy losses on Alexander, but finally in desperation they set fire to their houses and cast themselves into the flames along with their wives and children. The people of Malloi (Mālavas) and Oxydrakai (Kṣudrakas) faced him jointly with an army of 90,000 infantry, 10,000 cavalry and 900 elephants. In this battle Alexander suffered a grievous injury, and consequently the infuriated Greeks killed a large number of Mallois, including women and children.[29]

The army of Alexander also defeated a large army of Abastanoi (Ambaṣṭhas) comprising 60,000 infantry, 6,000 cavalry and 500 chariots. During the last phase of his withdrawal he defeated Xathroi (Kṣatri), Ossadioi (Vasāti), Sodrai (Śūdras), Massanoi, etc. Alexander also subjugated a number of rulers, viz., Mousikanos (Mūṣikas), Oxykanos, Sambos (Śambhu) and Brāhmanoi (Brāhmaṇas)[30] in the lower Indus Valley.

In this connection Romila Thapar appears to be right in concluding that 'the reliability of the figures from the classical sources can be questioned and the numbers may well be arbitrary and incorrect. It is most unlikely that they were accurate and more likely that they were attempts to project the immense opposition faced by Alexander and his success in meeting it'.[31]

MAURYAN CONQUESTS

After the retreat of Alexander, north-west India was again caught in political chaos. In eastern India the oppressive rule of the Nandas was greatly resented by the people. This provided Candragupta Maurya an opportunity to establish his rule over India. He first liberated the Indian territory under the occupation of the Greeks and then proceeded to defeat the Nandas. His empire comprised nearly the whole of India including parts of modern Tamil Nadu and Karnataka. In 305 BC he defeated Seleucus, the Greek ruler of western Asia, and forced him to part with the territories of Kabul, Kandahar, Herat and Baluchistan.[32] It is notable that the army of Candragupta comprised 600,000 infantry, 30,000 cavalry, 9,000 elephants, 8,000 chariots and a naval fleet.[33] But again the numbers are very much suspect.

Not much is known about the military achievements of his son Bindusāra. His grandson Aśoka first secured the throne by defeating his adversaries and then extended his influence over the border people like the Yavanas, Kambojas, Gandhāras, Bhojas, Andhras, etc. During his conquest of Kaliṅga, at least one lakh people were killed and one and a half lakh wounded. The death and destruction of war so much hurt Aśoka that he vowed not to wage war in his life time again. The reign of Aśoka ended in 232 BC but the Mauryan rule lingered for another fifty years.

In 184 BC Puṣyamitra Śuṅga, the *senāpati* of the last Mauryan king Bṛhadratha, put an end to Maurya rule.[34] He defeated Yajñasena, the ruler of Vidarbha and kept the invading Bactrian Greeks at bay.[35] He also inflicted defeat on a Greek ruler of India.[36]

Around 72 BC one Vāsudeva of Kaṇva family usurped the throne of Pāṭaliputra after deposing Devabhūti, the last Śuṅga king.[37] Kaṇvas ruled for 45 years. The last ruler of this dynasty was deposed by Simuka who founded the Sātavāhana rule. This was also the time when Khāravela, the Cedi ruler, was busy in conquests. He defeated the Sātavāhana ruler and subjugated Mūṣika, Rathika and Bhojaka kingdoms. He twice invaded Magadha, defeated a Yavana commander and vanquished a Pāṇḍyan king.[38]

Śātakarṇī, the son of Simuka, earned many victories and performed *Aśvamedha* sacrifice. Then started a long war for supremacy between the Śakas and the Sātavāhanas. In the first round the Śakas had the upper hand and they captured some Sātavāhana territories of Maharashtra. But Gautamīputra Śātakarṇī soon recaptured these territories from the Śakas. He also defeated Pallavas and some other Kṣatriya rulers.[39] The resurgence of Sātavāhanas was cut short by Rudradāman, the Śaka Kṣatrapa, who defeated Pulamāvi some time after AD 130.[40] But during the rule of Yajña Śrī Śātakarṇi (AD 165-95) Sātavāhanas retrieved their lost territories from the Śakas.[41] After him the disintegration of Sātavāhanas set in. Ābhīras occupied their western territories whereas Ikṣvākus and Pallavas grabbed their eastern possessions. Bitter fighting might have preceded the capitulation of Sātavāhanas.

FOREIGN INVASIONS (SECOND ROUND)

In third century BC taking advantage of the declining Seleucid power the rulers of Parthia and Bactria declared their independence. In 183 BC Demetrius, the Greek ruler of Bactria, crossed Hindukush and occupied parts of Punjab. He then marched through Sāketa, Pañcāla, and Mathurā and threatened Pāṭaliputra.[42] After him Eukratides, another Greek ruler, invaded India and became the master of 1,000 cities.[43] Menander, a scion of this family, also won many battles in India.[44] The successors of these Greek invaders came to be known as Indo-Greeks and they ruled over parts of western India till the first century AD.

In second century BC unfavourable political developments in Central Asia forced the Scythians to abandon their home. Overcoming the Greek and Parthian opposition on the way they reached India in second century BC. Maues, the Scythian leader, soon established his authority over Gandhāra and Punjab after defeating the Greek rulers.[45] Subsequently, four Scythian houses came to rule over

Taxila, Mathurā, Ujjain and Maharashtra. This could have been possible only after winning many battles. The Kṣaharātas, the Scythian royal house of Ujjayinī, fought a long drawn war with the Sātavāhanas. Nahapāṇa, Caṣṭana and Rudradāman also earned many victories in India.

This was also the time when Pahlavas of Iran turned towards India. Their ruler Vonones defeated the Śakas, established his power over Seistan and Kandahar and assumed the title of *Mahārājādhirāja*. Gondophernes, one of his successors, who ruled in early first century AD, assumed the titles *Mahārāja* and *Mahārājādhirāja*, perhaps after earning many victories.[46] After his death the Pahlavas were swept aside by the mighty Kuṣāṇas.

The Kuṣāṇas, a branch of the Yueh-chi tribe, then settled in Central Asia, invaded India in mid-first century AD. This invasion was led by Vima Kadphises, the son of Kujula Kadphises, who occupied Sindh, Punjab and parts of present-day Uttar Pradesh. His successor Kaniṣka conquered Sāketa and Magadha and repulsed an attack by the Pahlavas of Iran. He led an expedition to Central Asia and conquered Balkha, Kashgar, Khotan and Yarkand. His conquests thus included Kashmir, Sindh, Uttar Pradesh, Bihar and parts of Central Asia. He ruled over this vast empire from Peshawar. His successors Vāsiṣka and Huviṣka maintained the empire, but the disintegration started showing during the reign of Vāsudeva, when the territories of Central Asia, lower Indus Valley and eastern Mālwā slipped out. However, the final blow to the Kuṣāṇa power was struck by the Sassanians of Iran under the leadership of Ardashīr Bābagān (AD 225-41).

The decline of Kuṣāṇa power led to the emergence of many petty kingdoms in the country. Among them Nāgas emerged powerful and they performed as many as ten horse sacrifices to celebrate their victories.[47]

GUPTA CONQUESTS

The Nāgas could not maintain their supremacy for long and were replaced by the Guptas. As Śrīgupta and Ghaṭotkaca Gupta, two early rulers of the dynasty, were mere feudatories, it appears that Candragupta I (AD 320-35) put the family on the path of glory. He married a Licchavi princess and this added to his power and influence. He waged many wars, extended his kingdom to south Bihar, Prayāga, Sāketa and adjoining areas and assumed the title of *Mahārājādhirāja*.

Samudragupta (AD 335-75), the son of Candragupta I, was a great commander and his brave deeds are recorded in the Allahabad Pillar Inscription.[48] After ascending the throne he violently exterminated the nine kings of Āryāvarta. More than five bordering states and some tribal states accepted his authority. After an expedition to the south, he subjugated twelve rulers, and made them vassals. It seems that Kuṣāṇas, Śakas, Siṁhalas, etc., submitted before him and were in turn authorized to rule over their territories. After completing these victories Samudragupta performed an *Aśvamedha-yajña*.

Candragupta II (AD 375-414), the son of Samudragupta, not only maintained the large empire of his father, but also expanded it. He waged war against the Śakas, who were ruling over western India, and conquered Mālwā, Gujarat and Saurāṣṭra regions.

Kumāragupta I (AD 415-55) maintained the empire by suppressing revolts and defeating invaders. Puṣyamitras, the tribals who inhabited the banks of Narmadā were defeated by his son Skandagupta in a grim battle.[49] Skandagupta (AD 455-67) had to face Hūṇa invasion in AD 458 and though he was successful in defeating them they stayed around the borders. His successors Purugupta, Narasiṁhagupta, Kumāragupta III and Budhagupta maintained the empire despite internal revolts and external threats. Bhānugupta (AD 495-510), the last ruler of the dynasty, however, proved a weakling and was defeated by Toramāṇa, the Hūṇa chief.[50] Toramāṇa may have earned some more victories. His son Mihirakula is said to have crossed swords with Bālāditya of Magadha and Yaśodharman of Mālwā, though not successfully. King Yaśodharman claims to have earned more victories than the Gupta rulers.

VĀKĀṬAKA CONQUESTS

Vākāṭakas rose to power in the Bundelkhand region in the last quarter of the third century AD. Their empire included Bundelkhand, Central Provinces, Berar and Northern Deccan and some bordering states accepted their suzerainty. Pravarasena, the second ruler of the dynasty, performed as many as four *Aśvamedha-yajñas* and assumed the title of *Samrāṭ*. This suggests that he fought many successful battles. His grandson crossed swords with Samudragupta and was defeated. Guptas, however, craved friendship with them and Candragupta II married his daughter to a Vākāṭaka prince. King Harisеṇa waged successful wars against Kuntala, Avantī, Kaliṅga, South Kośala, Trikūṭa, Lāṭa and Andhra. In mid-sixth century the Vākāṭaka succumbed to the growing might of the Kalacuris.[51]

ROAD TO INSTABILITY

The disintegration of the Gupta empire led to the emergence of many petty kingdoms in northern India. Hūṇas established a kingdom in western India. Yaśodharman became powerful in Mālwā. Maitrakas established an independent kingdom in Valabhī. Later Guptas rose to power in Magadha and Śaśāṅkadeva came to rule over

Gauḍa (Bengal). Maukharis became all powerful in Kanauj. These dynasties remained in perpetual conflict with each other. The Maukharis and later Guptas fought a long drawn war which ended only with the killing of Maukhari king Grahavarman by Devagupta.

On the ruins of the Gupta empire also rose the Vardhanas of Thānesar. Prabhākaravardhana fought many successful battles with Hūṇas as also with the rulers of Sindh, Gurjara, Gandhāra and Lāṭa countries. His son Rājyavardhana defeated the Mālwā army and was in turn killed by Śaśāṅkadeva of Gauḍa. Harṣavardhana defeated the rulers of Valabhī and Sindh and his empire encompassed nearly the whole of northern India. Harṣa, however, suffered defeat at the hands of Cāḷukya king Pulakeśin II. The army of Harṣa is stated to have comprised sixty thousand elephants and one lakh horses, but again the numbers appear to be highly exaggerated.[52]

The death of Harṣa in AD 648 was followed by political instability in northern India. The throne of Kanauj was usurped by a minister of Harṣa. His cruelty towards a Chinese mission invited an invasion. Bhāskaravarman of Prāgjyotiṣa captured Karṇasuvarṇa. The feudatory ruler of Magadha, declared his independence and performed an *Aśvamedha-yajña.*

Though Kanauj continued as the centre of political activity, many independent states emerged in the country in eighth and ninth centuries. This led to many bloody wars. Rāṣṭrakūṭas of Mānyakheta, Pālas of Bengal and Āyudhas of Kanauj participated in a long drawn war. This finally led to the rise of Pratihāras in Kanauj.

SOUTH INDIAN WARS

The story of warfare in the south was no different.[53] It is believed that Candragupta Maurya had conquered and incorporated major parts of south India in his empire. In first century AD Sātavāhanas emerged as the most powerful dynasty in the Deccan. They fought a long drawn battle with the Śakas and tasted both victories and defeats. On the ruins of Sātavāhanas, the Ikṣvākus and Pallavas emerged as most powerful. In sixth century AD, Cāḷukya ruler Pulakeśin I, riding on the crest of victories against Maurya, Kadamba and Nala rulers, rose to power in the south. The weight of his arms was felt as far as Magadha and Bengal. He performed *Aśvamedha-yajña* to celebrate his victories. Pulakeśin II was the most powerful ruler of this dynasty. He conquered Kadamba, Anūpa, Maurya, Lāṭa, Mālwā and Gurjara rulers and repulsed the invasion of Harṣavardhana of Thānesar. The rulers of Kośala, Kaliṅga and Kāñcīpuram feared him. The Coḷas, Pāṇḍyas and Keralas submitted before his might. Pulakeśin II was killed during the invasion of Pallava ruler Narasiṁha-varman in AD 642 and it was the beginning of a long drawn war between the Pallavas and Cāḷukyas.

The Rāṣṭrakūṭas also fought many battles in the south. The arms of Dantidurga marched into Mahārāṣṭra, Kāñcī, Kaliṅga, Mālwā, Lāṭa, Ṭoṅka and Śrīśaila regions. His successors Kṛṣṇa II and Dhruva Nirupama were also great conquerors. The latter fought many battles with Coḷas, Pāṇḍyas, Pallavas, Gaṅgas, Keralas and humbled them. He also defeated the Cāḷukyas of Veṅgī, Pālas of Bengal and Pallavas of Kāñcī, besides many other petty kingdoms. Kṛṣṇa III was another great ruler of this dynasty. Internecine wars among the southern states continued till the Turk invaders conquered them one after another.

The history of ancient India has thus been crowded with wars. In the process Indians devised methods of dressing and equipping soldiers for better performance in the battlefield. The foreign invaders also contributed substantially in introducing now dress styles. In the following chapters the dress and accoutrements of soldiers in various periods of ancient Indian history has been described in detail.

NOTES

1. Irfan Habib, *The Indus Civilization*, pp. 60-1; Also see J. Marshall, *Mohenjo-daro and the Indus Civilization*, pp. 35-6.
2. *Ṛgveda*, 1.32.11, 1.51.6, 2.15.9, 2.20.7, 3.34.9, 6.25.2, 6.33.3, 6.60.6, etc.
3. Ibid., 1.51.6, 1.112.14, 2.19.6, 6.26.5, etc.
4. Ibid., 4.38.1, 7.19.3.
5. Ibid., 7.18.
6. Ibid.
7. Ibid.
8. Ibid., 7.18, 7.33.3.
9. Ibid., 7.18.19, 7.33.3.
10. *Aitareya Brāhmaṇa*, 1.14.
11. *Śatapatha Brāhmaṇa*, 1.14.
12. Ibid., 13.5.4.19-23.
13. This is evident from Brāhmaṇa literature, particulary the *Śatapatha Brāhmaṇa*, see Kāṇḍas 5 and 13.
14. R.S. Tripathi, *History of Ancient India*, p. 145.
15. *Mahābhārata* (*Mbh*), Sabhā, 47-8.
16. Ibid., Mausala, 8.9.
17. *Rāmāyaṇa* (*Rām*), Laṅkā Kāṇḍa.
18. R. Hiene-Geldren, *American Institute of Art and Archaeology*, vol. 5, 1937, p. 7.
19. S. Piggot, *Pre-historic India*, p. 238; also see Bridget and Raymond Allchin, *The Rise of Civilization in India and Pakistan*, p. 256.
20. Romila Thapar, *Early India*, p. 143.
21. D.N. Jha, *Early India: A Concise History*, pp. 55-6; also see Bridget and Raymond Allchin, op. cit., pp. 309-46.
22. *Aṅguttara Nikāya*, 1.213; 4.225, 256, 260.
23. Rhys Davids, *Buddhist India*, pp. 23-9.
24. Tripathi, op. cit., p. 119.

25. J.W. M'Crindle, *The Invasion of India by Alexander the Great*, pp. 221-2.
26. H.C. Raychaudhuri, *Political History of Ancient India*, pp. 187-90.
27. E.J. Rapson, *Cambridge History of India*, vol. 1, p. 348.
28. M'Crindle, op. cit., p. 270.
29. Ibid.
30. Ibid.
31. Romila Thapar, 'The Role of the Army in the Exercise of Power in Early India', p. 29 see *Army and Power in the Ancient World*, ed. Angelos Chaniotis and Pierre Ducrey.
32. V.A. Smith, *Early History of India* (4th edition), pp. 158-60.
33. Tripathi, op. cit., p. 151.
34. The event finds mention in Purāṇas also.
35. *Mahābhāṣya*, 3.2.111; also *Gārgī Saṁhitā*, *IHQ*, 1925, p. 215, etc.
36. *Mālavikāgnimitram*, Act 5, after *śloka* 14.
37. *Harṣacarita*, pp. 59-62.
38. *Epigraphia Indica*, vol. 20, pp. 80-1.
39. Ibid., vol. 8, pp. 60-1.
40. Ibid., pp. 36-49.
41. This is evident from the discovery of coins.
42. *Gārgī Saṁhitā*, op. cit.
43. W.W. Tarn, *Greeks in Bactria and India*, pp. 195-7.
44. Ibid., p. 225.
45. Stenkonow, *Journal of Indian History*, 1933.
46. *Corpus Inscriptionum Indicarum*, vol. V, intro., p. 37, etc.
47. Ibid., vol. 3, pp. 237, 241, 248, 425.
48. Ibid., pp. 1-17.
49. Ibid., pp. 53-5.
50. Ibid., pp. 146-8.
51. For details see K.A. Nilkanta Sastri, *A History of South India*.
52. T. Watters, *On Yuan Chwang's Travels in India*, vol. 1, p. 343.
53. For details see Sastri, op. cit.

CHAPTER 2

Military Costume: Determining Factors

The earliest recognition of fighting man's need for a distinctive costume is reflected in his effort to paint or stain his body with the intent to ward off danger and frighten the enemy. The use of leaves, barks, twigs, horns, hides and teeth and nails of ferocious animals as dress material can also be ascribed to the same impulse.

The costume and accoutrements have a direct bearing on the fighting capability of a soldier. Ancient Indians had definitely realized the truth. During the Mauryan times the state maintained a separate department to provide for the costume-related needs of the army. However, the factors like the large size of the country, variation in climatic conditions, and a heterogeneous social order militated against the uniform growth or standardization of military costume in India. Repeated foreign invasions and sharp regional differences also acted as impediments.

CLIMATIC FACTOR

Generally, the climatic conditions of a country determine the make and shape of the costume of its people. The inhabitants of cold climatic zones naturally use heavy and warm clothes. Their costume is so designed as to provide maximum protection to the body against the biting cold. The heavy coat and trousers worn by the people of the steppes, who invaded India from time to time, confirm this.

In hot climatic zones, on the other hand, people prefer light fabrics. The dress is so designed as to expose most of the body to allow air to cool it. The choice of traditional Indian costume of *adhovāsa*, *uttarīya* and *uṣṇīṣa* was obviously determined by the country's tropical climate.

It is understandable, therefore, that the invaders who generally came from colder climatic zones appeared on the Indian battlefield in heavy and warm costume, and were confronted by scantily dressed defenders. This difference in the costume of the invaders and the defenders might have been witnessed widely around the beginning of the Christian era when the Śaka-Kuṣāṇa invasions took place. The heavy costume of the invaders, originally intended as a protection against weather, may also have served the purpose of an armour, giving the wearer a better protection against an arrow-shot, spear-thrust or sword-cut.

Once the invaders settled down, heavy costume became a liability for them in the tropical Indian heat. It was gradually discarded and replaced by a lighter wear suited to Indian conditions. A comparison between the costume of the soldiers represented in the art of Gandhāra and Mathurā on the one hand and that of Ajantā on the other also confirms this. In no case the Śaka-Kuṣāṇas could have continued with their heavy costume for long. Presumably, the Āryans may also have undergone a similar experience some fifteen hundred years earlier.

DRESS MATERIAL

Next to climate it was the availability of dress material which determined the choice of costume for a people. The inhabitants of the Indus Valley used some kind of fabric for making garments as early as 2500 BC. According to Mackay:

though there is proof that cotton fabrics were used at Mohenjo-daro, there is at present no evidence of the use of linen or wool. The existence of linen cloth in Eleam at about the same date would suggest that it was also known at Mohenjo-daro and if not actually manufactured in the Indus Valley or elsewhere in ancient India, it may well have been imported like so many other things from Eleam or Sumer. It is uncertain whether wool was used, though sheep and goat could have provided an ample supply of raw material.[1]

In the context of the dress material used by the people of Mohenjo-daro Marshall says that:

For warmer textiles wool was used; for lighter ones, cotton. The cotton resembles the coarser varieties of present-day Indian cottons, and was produced from a plant closely related to *Gossypium arboreum* or one of its varieties. This discovery disposes finally of the idea that the fine Indian cotton known to the Babylonians as *sindhu* and to the Greeks as *sindon* was a product of the cotton-tree and not a true cotton.[2]

The Vedic Indians used wool for making garments is amply borne out by the allusions to weaving in the *Ṛgveda*.[3] The references to tanners and skins[4] suggest that skin was also used as dress material. Āryans, as a pastoral people, may have undoubtedly enjoyed abundant supply of skin.

The *Aṣṭādhyāyī* of Pāṇini refers to four types of fabrics that were used for making garments. These included *kauśeya* (silken cloth),[5] *auma* or *aumaka* (linen cloth),[6] *aurṇa* or *aurṇaka* (woollen cloth)[7] and *kārpāsa* (cotton cloth).[8]

In Buddhist Vinaya texts silk, wool, cotton and linen are said to be common fabrics.[9] In the Sūtra literature *kṣauma* (flax), *śaṇa* (hemp), *kārpāsa* (cotton) and *aurṇa* (wool) are mentioned as the main fabrics[10] but silk, barks and *kuśa* grass were also used.[11] The *Manusmṛti* refers to these fabrics[12] as also the wool made out of the hairs of cow, goat, sheep, etc.[13] The *Arthaśāstra* refers to wool, bark fibres, cotton, silk-cotton, hemp and flax as dress material.[14]

In the *Mahābhārata* various types of dress material are alluded to. During the *Rājasūya* sacrifice of Pāṇḍavas, Cīna, Śaka, Hārahūṇa and Haimavata rulers presented Yudhiṣṭhira with fabrics like *aurṇa, rāṅkava, kīṭaja, paṭṭaja, kuṭṭīkṛta, kārpāsa* and *ajina* produced in China and Bactria.[15] In another context clothes made of *kṣauma, kuśa, kauśeya, valkala, avika* and *carma* are mentioned.[16] Still at another place fabrics like *kṣauma, śāṇī, vāla, paṭṭa, falaka*, etc., and hides like *ajina, vyāghracarma* and *siṁhacarma* are mentioned.[17] Among these fabrics *dukūla, kṣauma* and *ajina* were particularly recommended for the use of Brāhmaṇas.[18] The unmarried men (*brahmacārins*) were advsied to use *kṣauma, kārpāsika* or *mṛgājina* as dress material.[19] The ascetics often used *carma* or *valkala.*[20]

The *Amarakośa* has classified the dress material in four categories, viz., *vālka, phāla, kauśeya* and *rāṅkava.* Of these *vālka* was made of bark. *Phāla* was made of the thread obtained from the fruits, including *kārpāsa. Kauśeya* was made of the thread produced by the silk worms. *Rāṅkava* was indeed made from the soft hair obtained from deer skin.[21] Ancient Indians thus appear to have used various fabrics, wools, skins barks, etc., as dress material. But it was the cotton which suited them the best for climatic reasons.

It thus appears that the Indus Valley people, who grew cotton, wore cotton cloths. The Āryans, who as a pastoral people enjoyed an abundant supply of skin and wool, used them for making apparel. However, the hot climatic conditions in India may have compelled the Āryans to discard their heavy wear and go for the lighter cotton. That the Āryans had changed over to cotton before the fifth century BC is evident from Brāhmaṇa and Sūtra literature and the Buddhist Jātakas. Indian soldiers of the Persian army, who fought against the Greeks in fifth century BC, were seen clad in cotton clothes. In fourth century BC again the Greeks found Indian soldiers dressed in cotton clothes.

The cotton thus remained the main fabric for making dress in India over the centuries. This might have necessitated large production of cotton in the country. There is an interesting reference to cotton cultivation in the Gangetic plains in a Buddhist Jātaka story.[22] There were cotton field in the vicinity of Banaras city and the women who looked after these fields were called *kapāsakhettarakṣikās.*[23]

In this context it is notable that the foreign invaders of India used woollens, silks and hides as dress material. In Indian literature the woollens are generally spoken of in relation to the people of foreign origin. *Cīnānśuka* and *cīnapaṭṭa* were indeed Chinese contribution to the Indian textile industry. *Stavaraka,* a heavy textile type, was introduced by the Iranians. Some varieties of skin such as *samūra, cīnasī,* and *sāmuli* were imported from Bactria to make shields and armour. Some kinds of skin like *kārdaraṅga* came from the South-East Asian region.[24]

Dyeing and Cleaning

Ancient Indians knew the art of dyeing cloth as early as the proto-historic times. The purple dye on a scrap of cotton material discovered at Mohenjo-daro has been indentified to be of madder class.[25] Dyed clothes were used in the Sūtra period and there are many references to garments dyed in red, yellow, saffron, and black colours in Sūtra literature.[26]

Pāṇini refers to several dyes, the cloth dyed being named after the dye (*ten raktam rāgāt*). *Rāga* signified both the colour and dye stuff. Cloth dyed with red colour was known as *lohitaka* and with black colour *kālaka*. *Lakṣa* was a popular commercial dye produced in India from very early times. Lacquer work was called *jātuṣa*. Madder (*mañjiṣṭha*), indigo (*nīla*) and orpiment (*rocanā*) were also known as dyes—a garment dyed in indigo was known as *nīlā*.[27]

The Buddhist Vinaya texts refer to dyes prepared from roots, trunks, barks, leaves, flowers, fruits, etc. The clothes were treated in a trough[28] to dye them in colours such as red, yellow, saffron and black.[29] In the *Mahābhārata* there are many references to dyeing.[30] The soliders often dressed in yellow, white, red or black garments.[31]

The Buddhist texts also refer to the method of cleaning unwashable cloths. It is said that silk and woollen garments were to be treated with alkaline earth, woollen blankets with powdered *ariṣṭa* fruit (soap berry tree), *aṁśupaṭṭa* with *bilva* fruit (bel) and linen cloth with the paste of yellow mustard.[32]

The *Arthaśāstra* describes the profession of dyeing in some detail. There was a class of craftsmen who were engaged in this work and rules had been framed to regulate their working, wages, etc. For any dispute concerning the work of dyeing, experts were called in to arbitrate.[33] Washermen were engaged to wash garments. They were expected to do washing in such a manner that the clothes were not damaged.[34]

Spinning and Weaving

According to B.C. Law 'The art of spinning, weaving and needle works developed in India in very early times'.[35] Cotton was spun and woven at Mohenjo-daro and probably also at Harappa. The numerous spindle whorls with rounded tops and flat, or slightly concave bases, found in both cities show that the women, if not the men, spent much of their spare time in spinning thread, which must assuredly have been cotton, for the majority of spindle-whorls are too small and light to spin elastic fibre like wool.[36] According to Marshall

> spinning was common in the houses of Mohenjo-daro is evident from the finding of numerous spindle-whorls in the houses; and that it was practised by the well to do and poor alike is indicated by the fact that the whorls are made of the more expensive faience as well as of the cheaper pottery and shell.[37]

The stone bust of a bearded man discovered at Mohenjo-daro appears wearing a *uttarīya.* Though the fabric of the *uttarīya* in difficult to identify it was certainly a woven cloth (Figure 1).

In the *Ṛgveda* there are many references to weaving suggesting that it had developed as an art in Vedic times. The following extracts confirm this:

(i) Weaving the raiment of the sheep and making raiment beautiful (*Ṛgveda,* 10.26.6).
(ii) They sit beside the warp and cry, weave forth, weave back (*Ṛgveda* 10.130.1).
(iii) They made the *Sāma* hymns their weaving shuttles (*Ṛgveda* 10.130.2).
(iv) What was spread out she weaves afresh, reweaving (*Ṛgveda,* 2.38.4).
(v) Good work for us, the glorious Night and Morning, like female weavers waxen from aforetime (*Ṛgveda,* 2.3.6).
(vi) Rats devour the weaver's thread (*Ṛgveda,* 1.105.8).

These allusions do not, however, present the detailed process of weaving. But a passage in the *Atharvaveda* gives some details while describing how night and day, personified as sisters, weave the web of the year alternately with thread that never breaks or comes to an end.[38] In the later Vedic literature[39] and Buddhist Pāli texts also there are numerous references to weaving.[40]

Figure 1: Statue (Warrior) Mohenjo-daro

The *Arthaśāstra* deals with the subject in some detail. It says that superintendent of yarn (*sūtrādhyakṣa*) 'should get yarn spun out of wool, bark-fibres, cotton, silk-cotton, hemp and flax through widows, crippled women, maiden women who have left their homes'.[41] Mills were established for 'the weaving of (cloth from) *kṣauma*, *dukūla*, silk yarn, hair of the *raṅku* deer, and cotton yarn thus produced by the workmen'.[42] Further, 'he should cause ropes to be made of yarn and fibres, (and) thongs of canes and bamboos, as trappings for war and bindings for vehicles and draught animals'.[43] In the *Rāmāyaṇa*, the experienced spinner is called *sūtrakarmaviśeṣajña*.[44] In the *Mahābhārata* a person who wove the cloth with the help of a needle is called *vāyaka*.[45] In the *Manusmṛti* the person who could weave cloth from various fabrics like cotton, flax, wool, etc., was called *tantuvāya*.[46]

Art of Sewing

It is believed that the art of sewing was known to Indians in the proto-historic times.[47] In the Vedic age *kavaca* and *varman* which denoted some kind of armour could not have been made without the knowledge of sewing. According to B.C. Law 'A Vedic Indian stands before us perfectly well dressed, caring for his dress and creating an art of making dress'.[48] R.L. Mitra adds that:

> the existence of such words as needle (*sūcī*) and sewing (*sivan*) in the Vedic language cannot be accounted for except on the supposition that the people who used them, knew and had what they meant. It may also be argued that it is very unlikely that the heroes of the Vedic times, who were able to forge and were in the habit of using armour and mail coats, never came to the idea of fashioning their clothes into made dresses.[49]

In the Brāhmaṇa and Sūtra literature, needle and needle works are referred.[50] In the *Aṣṭādhyāyī* there are indications that stitched garments were worn by people.[51] In the *Mahābhāṣya* there is a specific reference to needle and sewing.[52] In the *Rāmāyaṇa sūcī* is described as a sharp pointed device.[53] In the *Mahābhārata* a kind of battle-array has been called as *Sūcī-vyūha.*[54]

In the *Rāmāyaṇa*, the profession of tailor is called *tannavāya.*[55] But knowing that jackets and trousers like sewn garments were unknown to Indians, during the Vedic and epic times C.V. Vaidya observes that:

> we are tempted even to think that the art of cutting the cloth and sewing it into different kind of cloths was not known in the beginning of the epic period. Tailoring was an art probably of Semetic origin and was introduced into India about the time of Greek conquest of the Punjab or if at all earlier, at the time of Darius and in consequence of the contact of the Indo-Aryans with the Persians. Strange as it may sound, we find that the *Mahābhārata* makes no mention of a tailor.[56]

Though Indians may have used some kind of sewn garments from the earliest times it is certain that foreign invaders like Greeks, Śakas and Kuṣāṇas contributed substantially in popularizing such garments.[57] In this context the following observations by Altekar are significant:

> The introduction of sewn garments in India during the Kuṣāṇa period on an extensive scale influenced the costume of those who came in close contact with the court. The servants, both male and female, wore well-cut tunics and at times shorts. A minority of this class was probably of foreign origin, but the majority wearing the sewn garments were Indians.... The adoption of sewn garments by the horse-riders and a section of soldiers of the Gupta period also reveals Śaka influence.[58]

ECONOMIC CONDITIONS

The costume of the soldiers also reflected the economic health of a country. If the country was prosperous, soldiers dressed lavishly and wore costly ornaments. The costume also indicated the status of the warrior in the society. Senior commanders generally fought mounted on chariots and elephants and dressed elegantly as borne out by the epics and the art of Sāñcī and Ajantā. The infantry soldiers generally dressed scantily.

There was no major difference between the garment of a soldier and a civilian in ancient India. In fact, it was the mode of wearing which made the difference. To illustrate, *dhotī*, the common lower garment of Indians, was worn by soldiers in a style so that it did not impede the movement. In this *sakaccha* style the loose ends of the *dhotī* were carried between the legs and tucked behind. The civilians, however, left the ends of the *dhotī* loose to hang between the legs.

The use of skirt or kilt and a tight fitting tunic by soldiers at Sāñcī suggests Greek influence. The waist-band was a common wear but soldiers tied it in many folds which added to their smartness. The turban gave protection against the sun as also against the sword attack.

MILITARY TACTICS

The military tactics followed by a people in war also have a bearing on their costume and choice of vehicles. To illustrate, a people who followed the tactics of surprise and deception in war could not afford to fight with chariots or elephants. Cavalry and infantry alone could suit them. In the battle of Jhelum (326 BC) the Greeks with their fast moving infantry and cavalry inflicted a crushing defeat on Indians who mainly depended on chariots and elephants. The Indian long bow also lost its credibility in this battle and was soon replaced by a shorter one.

The Indian soldier mounted on chariot or elephant could don loose garments like *dhotī* and *uttarīya* but the Śaka-

Kuṣāṇa cavalryman could ill afford such garments. Quite naturally, they had invented an ingenious piece of cloth called trousers, which was convenient for fighting from the horseback. They had also invented a proper saddle and stirrup for a better balance on horseback. As a result of Śaka-Kuṣāṇa impact Indian soldiers also adopted new dress patterns and accoutrements. Interestingly, after settling in India the foreign invaders also adopted the Indian way of fighting and equipping.

FOREIGN INFLUENCE

Around the beginning of the Christian era foreign invaders like Greeks, Śakas and Kuṣāṇas influenced the Indian military costume and accoutrements considerably. A sculptured warrior at Bhārhut is represented in a typically un-Indian costume. In the Sāñcī art some soldiers wearing kilt and a tightly fitted half-sleeved skirt suggest Greek influence. The trousers and coats as also the stirrup and saddle for horses were introduced by the Śaka-Kuṣāṇas. The horse now became the principal vehicle of war, replacing the chariot and elephant indeed.

SOCIAL BINDINGS

The social set-up and religious leanings of a people also influence their dress style. The upper caste people like brāhmaṇas and kṣatriyas perhaps dressed more gorgeously than other caste people. This might have also reflected in their hair-do. The use of *candana*, *tilaka* and ornaments may have been exclusive to high-born warriors.

In this connection it is noteworthy that the nature of Indian costume was gravitational as it did not tune-up with the body structure and fell down loosely. Indian *adhovāsa*, *uttarīya*, and *uṣṇīṣa* all conform to this principle. But this dress style was not suitable for soldiers as it hampered movement and speed. As against this, the foreign invaders donned a costume which was in accord with body anatomy. To illustrate the point, the Śaka-Kuṣāṇas dressed in coat, trousers and caps or helmets, all anatomical in nature. This dress style was particularly suited to cavalry soldiers.

Thus many factors influenced the choice of military costume used by a people. These included the climate, military tactics, social set-up, religious beliefs, foreign contacts, etc. In the following chapters an effort has been made to picture the military costume and accoutrements used by the Indians during various periods of their history.

NOTES

1. E. Mackay, *Early Indus Civilization*, p. 79.
2. J. Marshall, *Mohenjo-daro and the Indus Civilization*, pp. 32-3.
3. *Ṛgveda*, 10.26.6, 10.130.1, 2.38.4, 2.3.6.
4. A.A. Macdonell, *A History of Sanskrit Literature*, p. 168.
5. *Aṣṭādhyāyī*, 6.3.42.
6. Ibid., 4.3.150.
7. Ibid., 4.3.158.
8. Ibid., 4.3.143.
9. *Sacred Books of the East*, vol. 25, p. 190; also E.B. Cowell, *The Jātaka*, 6.47.
10. *Gobhila Gṛhya-Sūtra*, 2.10.210.
11. Ram Gopal, *India of Vedic Kalpasūtras*, p. 156.
12. *Manusmṛti*, 3.41, 44; 4.66; 5.120; 8.326; 10.87; 11.167, 169; 12.64.
13. Ibid., 2.44; 5.120.
14. *Arthaśāstra*, 2.23.2.
15. प्रमाणरागस्पर्शाढ्यं बाह्लीकचीनसमुद्भवम्।
    और्णं च राङ्कवं चैव कीटजं पट्टजं तथा।
    कुट्टीकृतं तथैवान्यत्कमलाभं सहस्रशः।
    श्लक्ष्णं वस्त्रमकार्पासमाविंक मृदु चाजिनम्।। *Mahābhārata* (*Mbh*), Sabhā, 47.22-23.

16. क्षौमं च कुशचीरं च कौशेयं वल्कलानि च।
आविकं चर्म च समं यस्य स्यान्मुक्त एव सः।। *Mbh*, Śānti, 277.35.
17. मुञ्जमेखलनग्नत्वं क्षौमकृष्णाजिनानि च।।
शाणीवालपरीधानो व्याघ्रचर्म परिच्छदः।
सिंहचर्मपरीधानः पट्टवासास्तथैव च।।
कीटकावसनश्चैव चीरवासास्तथैव च।
वस्त्राणि चान्यानि बहून्यभिमन्यत्य बुद्धिमान्।। Ibid., Śānti, 292.11-13.
18. समं येषां दुकूलं च तथा क्षौमाजिनानि च। Ibid., Anuśāsana, 151.14 (BE).
19. क्षौमं कार्पासिकं चापि मृगाजिनमथापि वा। Ibid., Āśvamedhika, 46.5 (BE).
20. चर्मवल्कलसंवीतः। Ibid., 46.10.
21. *Amarakośa*, 2.6.111.
22. E.B. Cowell, *The Jātaka*, 3.286.
23. Ibid., 6.286
24. For details see U.P. Thapliyal, *Foreign Elements in Ancient Indian Society*, pp. 50, 51.
25. Marshall, op. cit., p. 33.
26. Ram Gopal, *India of Vedic Kalpasūtras*, pp. 158-9.
27. V.S. Agrawala, *India as Known to Pāṇini*, pp. 230-1.
28. *Mahāvagga*, 7.10.1.
29. Ibid., 8.29.1.
30. विरक्तं शोध्यते वस्त्रं न तु कृष्णोपसंहितम्। *Mbh.*, Śānti, 280.10.
लोहितैः सिच्यमानानि शस्त्राणि कवचानि च।
महारङ्गानुरक्तानि वस्त्राणीव चकाशिरे।। Ibid., Karṇa, 19.68.
वासो यथा रंगवशं प्रयाति। Ibid., Śānti, 288.33; also 280.10.
31. *Mbh*, Droṇa, 127.16.
32. *Sacred Books of the East*, vol. 25, p. 190.
33. *Arthaśāstra*, 4.1.18-21.
34. रजकाः काष्ठफलकश्लक्ष्णशिलासु वस्त्राणि नेनिज्युः। Ibid., 4.1.14.
35. B.C. Law, *Indological Studies*, vol. 1, p. 113.
36. Mackay, op. cit., pp. 90-1.
37. Marshall, op. cit., p. 32.
38. Macdonell, op. cit., p. 168.
39. Macdonell and Keith, *Vedic Index*, vol. 1, pp. 298-9.
40. Moti Chandra, *Prācīna Bhāratīya Veśa-bhūṣā*, p. 26.
41. *Arthaśāstra*, 2.23.2, also 23.11-12; It is notable that the work of spinning and weaving was entrusted to women even in Vedic times (*Atharvaveda*, 10.7.42, 14.2.51).

42. Ibid., 2.23.8-10; also 4.1.8-13.
43. *Arthaśāstra*, 2.23.19; also 4.1.8.
44. *Rām* (*Rāmāyaṇa*), Ayodhyā, 83.12.
45. सूच्या सूत्रं यथा वस्त्रे संसारयति वायकः । *Mbh*, Śānti, 210.34.
46. *Manusmṛti*, 3.31, 44; According to the *Amarakośa*, weavers were called *tantuvāya* and *kuvinda*. *Amar*, 2.10.6.
47. Mackay, op. cit., pp. 90-1.
48. Law, op. cit., vol. 4, p. 24.
49. R. Mitra, *Indo-Aryans*, p. 178.
50. *Śatapatha Brāhmaṇa*, 12.7.2.11; Ram Gopal, op. cit., p. 138.
51. Agrawala, op. cit., pp. 126-7.
52. तीक्ष्ण्या सूच्या सीव्यान्, *Mahābhāṣya*, 2.92.
53. *Ram*, Vana, 46.41.
54. *Mbh*, Bhīṣma, 19.3-5, Droṇa, 63.23.
55. *Ram*, Ayodhyā, 83.15; तन्नवाय: सौचिक:। *Amarakośa*, 2.10.6.
56. C.V. Vaidya, *Epic India*, vol. 1, p. 141.
57. For details see Thapliyal, op. cit., pp. 52-62.
58. A.S. Altekar, *The Catalogue of the Gupta Gold Coins in the Bayana Hoard*, p. cliii.

CHAPTER 3

Harappan Age

It is generally believed that the authors of Indus Valley civilization were a people of peaceful demeanor. But in the creation and preservation of this great civilization some kind of organized force must have been used. According to Wheeler:

> it is to be supposed that the wide extent of the civilization was initially the product of something forcible than peaceful penetration. True this military element does not loom large amongst the extant remains but it must be remembered that at present we know nothing of the earliest phase of civilization.[1]

MILITARY DISPOSITION

The military disposition of the Indus Valley people is suggested by some archaeological evidence:

> At some of the Harappan sites, small rooms adjacent to a bigger structure have been called 'guard-rooms'. Barrack-like structures have been indentified at Lothal, Mohenjo-daro and Harappa. Further, if the Harappans really colonized the peripheral areas outside the Indus Valley proper as stated by Sankalia (1973) we cannot but think of a series of garrisoned and fortified outposts to hold the colonies under control. The excavations of J.P. Joshi (1974) at Surkotada in Kutch have brought to light a structure which, according to him, was a defence complex.[2]

Significantly, some male heads discovered at Harappa and Mohenjo-daro have been identified as warrior types.[3]

WEAPONS AND ACCOUTREMENTS

It was mainly the weapon which distinguished a soldier. A double-edged, thick, and blunt-pointed copper sword was the most popular weapon of the age.[16] According to Mackay 'the very substantial sword (pl. 119.9) is surprising at so early a date; it shows that at all events some of the people of Mohenjo-daro were well armed'.[17]

The bow was another popular weapon is suggested by the discovery of a large number of arrow-heads. These are thin, flat pieces of copper or bronze with sharp barbs and no tang. The shafts in which the arrow-heads were set must also have served as a kind of mid-rib.[18] These might have been fixed to a split bamboo or wooden shaft.[19]

Daggers and knives were also in vogue. According to Mackay:

> no sheath for either knives or daggers has yet been found. Whether wood or leather or some woven material, none could have survived the dampness or salinity of the soil. We do not even know how these weapons were carried; it may have been in a belt or perhaps under the arm.... Those of the blades which are too long to have been carried in the better manner must have been slipped in a belt, though we have no evidence from seal or statues of the wearing of such an article of clothing by males.[20]

Mace-heads of stone were certainly used as weapons by the soldiers of Mohenjo-daro as these have been found in large numbers and in various types.[21]

The discovery of a large number of sling-pellets suggests that the soldiers also carried a sling. It was essentially a weapon for open country and in the hands of a skilled man could prove formidable. Quite possibly it was introduced into India from the West, and at a very early period, as the specimen from Mohenjo-daro prove.[22] Spears and lances were also used.[23]

Perhaps, soldiers donned some kind of protective device like scale armour.[24] According to Pant, fabric armour was used in India at least in 2500 BC, during the Harappan age, if not before, and its use continued thereafter.[25] While marching to the battlefield soldiers carried their standards aloft (Figure 2).

Figure 2: Soldiers carrying standards

The military costume of the Harappans thus appears to have comprised a loin-cloth, a head-band, and some kind of protective body armour. They carried weapons like sword, bow, mace, javelin, etc.

NOTES

1. M. Wheeler, *The Cambridge History of India*, Supplementary Volume, p. 72.
2. Y.M. Citalwala, *Frontiers of the Indus Civilization*, ed. B.B. Lal, pp. 212-13.
3. Ibid., p. 213.
4. J. Marshall, *Mohenjo-daro and the Indus Civilization*, p. 282.
5. Ibid.
6. *Ṛgveda*, 1.130.7; 1.61.5; also 2.20.7-8; 3.12.6; 4.27.1, 4.30.20.
7. E.J.H. Mackay, *Further Excavations at Mohenjo-daro*, vol. 1, pp. 441, 591-2.
8. Ibid., p. 416.
9. E.J.H. Mackay, *Early Indus Civilization*, p. 80.

10. Mackay, *Further Excavations at Mohenjo-daro*, vol. 2, pl. 76.16.
11. Ibid., pls. 72.8-10; 76.6.
12. Ibid., pl. 75.16.
13. Ibid., Seals 222, 235, 420.
14. Ibid., Seal, 430; pl. 99A.
15. Ibid., p. 476.
16. Marshall, op. cit., vol. 1, p. 35; But Marshall is reluctant to accept the identification of this weapon as sword.
17. E.J.H. Mackay, *Further Excavations of Mohenjo-daro*, vol. 1, p. 442; also pp. 461-2.
18. Ibid., p. 461.
19. Ibid., pp. 461-2; also Marshall, op. cit., p. 499.
20. Ibid., p. 462; Marshall, op. cit., pp. 499-500.
21. Marshall, op. cit., p. 459.
22. Ibid., p. 467.
23. Ibid., p. 497; also p. 457.
24. Ibid., p. 546; also, pl. 143.19, p. 533.
25. G.N. Pant, *Indian Arms and Armour*, p. 3.

CHAPTER 4

Vedic Age

The Vedic soldiers dressed in some kind of costume and carried weapons which distinguished them from others. Many references in Vedic literature, particularly those relating to the Maruts, attest to this.

Who shine self-luminous with ornaments and sword, with breastplates, armlets and with wreaths. Arrayed on chariots and with bows. *Ṛgveda*, 5.53.4

Lances on your shoulders, anklets on your feet, gold chains are on your breasts, gems, Maruts, on your car.
Lightnings aglow with flame are flashing in your hand, and visors wrought of gold are laid upon your heads.
Ibid., 5.54.11

Armed with your daggers, full of wisdom, armed with spears, armed with your quivers, armed with arrows, with good bows, good horses and good cars have ye, O Pṛśni's sons: ye Maruts, with good weapons go to victory. Ibid., 5.57.2

Elsewhere, Maruts are described as adorning their person[1] and dazzling heaven and earth by their brightness,[2] which none else could match.[3] When dressed in deer skin and bearing a shield they created terror in enemy camps.[4] In another hymn they are described as clothed in robes of wool.[5] In another context they are described as bearing close resemblance to each other like twins.[6] This suggests that the Vedic soldiers generally dressed in a uniform pattern.

DRESS ITEMS

In any case the dress of a soldier may not have been very different from others. About the general dress of the people the *Vedic Index* has to say the following:

> The Vedic Indians seem often to have worn three garments—an undergarment (cf. *nivi*), a garment, and an over-garment (cf. *adhivāsa*) which was presumably a mantle, and for which names *atkah* and *drāpi* also seem to be used. This accords with the description of the sacrificial garments given in the *Śatapatha Brāhmaṇa* which comprise a *tārpya*, perhaps a 'silken undergarment'; secondly, a garment of undyed wool, and then a mantle, while the ends of the turban, after being tied behind the neck, are brought forward and tucked away in front.[7]

In the *Ṛgveda* the words *vāsas*, *vasanà*, or *vastra* refer to garments in general.[8] Some of these were perhaps stitched as the Āryans knew the art of sewing.[9] It appears that the male dress in the Vedic age comprised a *nīvi* (loin-cloth), a *vāsas*, and an *adhivāsa*.

BODY ARMOUR

A tight-fitting coat like garment called *drāpi*, was perhaps the main constituent of a soldier's costume.[10] The word *varma* widely occurring in the *Ṛgveda* denoted body armour, coat of mail, or corselet.[11] 'The corselet was not a single solid piece of metal but consisted of many pieces fitted together (*syūta*). It may have been made either of metal plates or, as is more likely, of some stiff material plated with metal.'[12] It could have also been made by sewing together pieces of skin as a skin garment was in common use among the Āryans.[13] The look and make of an armour is indicated in the following hymn:

> The warrior's look is like a thunderous rain-cloud's, when, armed with mail, he seeks the lap of battle.

Be thou victorious with unwounded body: so let the thickness of thy mail protect thee.[14]

Also

Thy vital parts I cover with thine armour: with immortality king Soma clothe thee.[15]

It seems that the garments made of deer-skin distinguished a warrior from other caste people.[16] In a particular reference to Maruts it is stated that by donning a deer-skin they caused terror among the enemy ranks.[17] It is also said that an armoured warrior can vanquish an unarmoured adversary easily and can inflict serious injuries.[18]

In the later Vedic literature there are many references to armour. In the *Atharvaveda* the word *kavaca* denoted a corselet or breast-plate.[19] In the *Vājasaneyī Saṁhitā* Rudra is described as 'girt in cotton-quilted cuirass'.[20] In the Sūtras a warrior is expected to wear his armour only after it has been sanctified by *mantras*.[21] The Vedic terms *varma* and *kavaca* have been translated as armour indiscriminately, but in reality these could not have meant one and the same thing. In the *Yajurveda*, Rudra is spoken of as wearing *kavaca* and *varma* both.[22]

In this context the word *atka* which is interpreted to mean breast-plate also deserves mention.

Maruts have been described as wearing golden breast-plates (*hiraṇmayān atkān* Rv. 5.55.6) which could be donned and doffed at pleasure. Zimmer explains the word elsewhere (Rv. 10.49.3; 99.9) as the 'armour of a warrior as a whole'. In other passages it is rendered garment, because it is said to be woven (*vyuta* Rv. I.122.2) or 'well-fitting' (*surabhi*, Rv. 6.29.3; 10.123.7).[23]

Regarding the use of armour in the Vedic age the observations of S.D. Singh are significant:

The use of protective armour is evidenced in the *Ṛgveda* as well as the later texts. The common word denoting a coat of mail in the *Ṛgveda* is *varman.* There are references to the sewing of the armour though the material of which it was made has not been specified. It may have been in the form of a linen or leather corselet reinforced with metal. A passage of the *Ṛgveda* speaks of a mailed warrior falling before the arrows like bursting vessels. Whatever it was made of, leather or metal or both, the armour of the early Āryans must have afforded ample protection against the weapons of the day. A later passage mentions corselets of *ayas, loha,* or *rajata.*[24] But not many people could have afforded the use of such expensive armour.

HELMET

Śipra was another important item of dress for a soldier.[25] It is variously interpreted to mean a turban, a cap, or a helmet. Perhaps, it was a kind of turban used to protect the head from a sword attack. The references to *ayas-śipra,*[26] *hiraṇya-śipra,*[27] and *hari-śipra*[28] in the *Ṛgveda* suggest that it was made of metal. A person donning *śipra* was known as *śiprin.*[29] According to Das 'In whatever sense the word may have been used, there can be no doubt that even in Ṛgvedic times metal helmets or visors were used by warriors for the protection of their head and face.'[30]

BRACE

The brace or guard was worn by the charioteers on the left arm, fastened on with leather straps. 'It encompasses the arm with serpent windings, fending away the friction of the bowstring.'[31]

WEAPONS

Much more than the dress it was the weapon and equipment which distinguished a soldier. The principal weapon of a Vedic soldier was the bow (*dhanuṣ*). It was 'composed of a stout staff bent into a curved shape (*vakra*) and of a bow string (*jyā*), made of a strip of cowhide, which joined the ends. The tips of the bow, where the string was fastened, were called *ārtni*. Relaxed when not in actual use, the bow was specially strung up when needed for shooting.'[32]

No warrior ever went out without the bow and parted company with it only when dead. The last act of the funeral rite of an Āryan required the removal of the bow from the right hand of the dead man.[33] The warriors beseeched the bow to grant them victories: 'with bow let us win kine, with bow the battle, with bow be victors in our hot encounters. The bow brings grief and sorrow to the foemen: armed with the bow may we subdue all regions.'[34]

The arrow (*iṣu*) was an integral part of the bow. It comprised a shaft (*śalya*), a feather-socket (*parṇa-dhi*) and a metal-head (*ayo-mukham*). The shaft was made of reed, a kind of grass, called *sara*. It was fastened with feathers to gain speed. The arrow-head was made of iron or some other metal. Length of an arrow was generally about five span or say three feet.[35] A Ṛgvedic hymn dedicated to arrows says: 'Her (arrow's) tooth a dear, dressed in an eagle's feathers, bound with cow-hide launched forth, she flieth onward.'[36] Griffith explains that 'the point of the arrow is made of a piece of deer's horn attached to the shaft with leather strings. The butt of the arrow is feathered.'[37] The shaft of the arrow made of reed was smeared with venom.[38] Though the bow was the main weapon of the Āryan soldier, the sword (*pavīra, asi, kārpāṇa*), lance (*sṛka, śakti*), axe (*paraśu*), thunderbolt (*vajra*), etc., were also known.[39]

ACCOUTREMENTS

The arrows were carried in a quiver called *iṣudhi* or *niṣaṅga*. Archers carried it on their back on the right side.[40] A Vedic

Plate 2: Vedic soldier

hymn dedicated to the quiver runs: 'Flung on the back, pouring his brood, the quiver vanquishes all opposing bands and armies'.[41]

A hand-guard (*hastaghna*) made of leather protected the left hand from the impact of the bow-string.[42] A reference to *khādi* in the *Ṛgveda* has been interpreted to mean a protective device for hands.[43]

Some kind of leg-guard may also have been in vogue. According to Das:

> There is also no clear record of the employment of greaves or other guards for the legs and feet, but Grassmann saw greaves in *vatūriṇā padā* in Rv.1.133.2. It would certainly be strange if there were no greaves or guards for the legs and feet, when the body was protected by armour or coat of mail, the head and face by helmet or visor, and the arm by *hastaghna*.[44]

Paṭsaṅginī referred to in the *Atharvaveda*[45] also appears to have been a kind of leg-guard, used by foot-soldiers. *Khādi* was another piece of equipment, for the protection of legs.[46] *Upānaha* was a kind of shoe, which came into vogue in the later Vedic age.[47] Elkazi comments that 'the shoes in the early Vedic age, had been worn only during rituals, and by soldiers'.[48]

In the *Ṛgveda*, some items of equipment such as *añji*, *rukma*, *vāsī*, *sṛja* and *niṣka* are mentioned in relation to Maruts. In a hymn the *gaṇa* (formation) of Maruts is stated to be adorned with *rukma* and *añji*.[49] Another hymn says that *rukma* was worn over the chest.[50] Perhaps, it was a bright piece of metal, worn on chest as a protective device.

The *añji*, was another piece of equipment borne on the body.[51] Perhaps, it was worn over the shoulders as a protective device like *rukma* on the chest.

The *varūtha* (shield) was used as a protective device.[52] The Maruts carried with them the shields made of deer-skin.[53]

Vāsī was another piece of equipment which finds mention in relation to Maruts.[54] Das has interpreted it as a carpenter's hatchet which was used as a weapon by the Maruts.[55] But repeated allusion to *vāsī* in the *Ṛgveda* suggests that it was an important piece of equipment like *rukma* and *añji.*

These equipments have been interpreted as some kind of ornament. According to Das *niṣka* was a golden ornament worn on the neck, *rukma* was another golden ornament worn on the breast, *sṛja* was a garland and *khādi* a golden anklet or an armlet.[56] But to begin with these decorative devices must have served some real purpose in a war. In the later Vedic period warriors wore an amulet tied to their hand by the priest,[57] perhaps assuring them safety in war.

DHVAJA

The *dhvaja* (standard) formed an integral part of military accoutrement in the Vedic age.[58] All soldiers carried a *dhvaja* and those who could not afford it borrowed one before joining a battle.[59] Perhaps, it was the symbol of Indra, the Āryan god of war, as suggested by a Vedic hymn. 'When the standards meet together (or when the battle starts) at that time Indra (*dhvaja*) may be our defender.'[60] There is also a reference to targeting of the enemy standard.[61] A hymn addressed to *dhvaja* gives some indication of its shape and make. 'The chanters hymn thee, they who say the word of praise magnify thee. The priests have raised thee up on high, O Śatakratu, like a pole.'[62] Perhaps, this symbol of Indra was a replica of *sūrya* (sun).[63]

VRĀTYA COSTUME

In the later Vedic literature a particular dress pattern is mentioned in respect of the Vrātya people of India. Their leaders used a black bordered white turban and a coat made of goat-skin of black or white hue. A garland adorned the neck. The soldiers wore a red bordered skin-coat designed after the garment of their leader.[64] In Sūtra literature the Vrātyas are described as dressed in red turban[65] and garments (*vāsas* and *urapaṭṭa*) of white and red cloth.[66] Incidentally, this type of costume is nowhere mentioned in relation to the Āryans. Thus the Vrātya people dressed and equipped their soldiers better than the Āryans.

MILITARY VEHICLES

The vehicles of war, viz., chariot, elephant and horse constituted an integral part of military paraphernalia. It is said that Sumerian people had invented the wheeled vehicle around fourth millennium BC and that the Āryans borrowed it from them around two millennium BC. They improved upon it by adding spokes to the wheel, doing away with two of the four wheels, and substituting horse for the ass.[67] The Vedic chariot carried two persons, viz., the fighter and the driver.[68]

Chariot and Horse

The main components of the chariot included *kośa* (box of the chariot), *Akṣa* (wooden axle to which the box was fastened by a strap of cow-hide), *cakra* (wheels), *yuga* (yoke) and *nemi* (rim). In the *Ṛgveda* Bhṛgus, a people who rose to priesthood subsequently, appear as chariot makers.[69] In the *Atharvaveda rathakārāḥ* (chariot makers) appear as a functional caste.[70] The *Vedic Index* sketches a Vedic chariot as follows:

> Normally there was, it seems one pole, on either side of which the horses were harnessed, a yoke (*yuga*) being laid across their necks; the pole was passed through the hole in the yoke (called

kha or *tardman*), the yoke and the pole being then tied together.... The horses were tied by the neck (*grīvā*) where the yoke was placed, and also at the shoulder, presumably by traces fastened to a bar of wood at right angles to the pole, or fastened to the ends of the pole, if that is to be regarded, as it probably should, as of triangular shape, wide at the foot and coming to a point at the tip. The traces seem to be denoted by *raśmi* and *raśanā*. These words also denote the reins, which were fastened to the bit (perhaps *śiprā*) in the horse's mouth. The driver controlled the horses by reins and urged them on with a whip (*kaśā*). The girths of the horse were called *kakṣya*.[71]

Chariots were painted in various colours such as red (*aruṇa*) and red-brown (*piṣaṅga*).[72] The wheels were worked in gold or in golden hue.[73]

Earlier, it was believed that the horse was not used as a vehicle of war during the Vedic period. Macdonell says that in Vedic literature 'no mention is made of riding in battle'.[74] Keith confirms this while stating that 'though horse-riding was probably not unknown for other purposes, no mention is made of the use of the horse in war'.[75] According to Chakravarti 'there is no satisfactory record of the use of cavalry in a battle of that period'.[76] But in the *Ṛgveda* a hymn addressed to Maruts seems to dispel this belief:

O heroes lordiest of all, who are ye that have singly come forth from a region most remote?

Where are your horses, where are reins? How came ye: How had ye the power? Rein was on nose and seat on the back. The whip is laid upon the flank.

The heroes stretch their thighs apart.[77]

It follows that in the Vedic age the equipment of the horse included rein, whip and some kind of saddle. Elsewhere, it is stated that the legs of the horse bore ornaments of gold.[78] Perhaps, the elephant was also used in war.

It seems that the Indians had devised some kind of military costume in the Vedic age. The soldiers could be distinguished by their dress, armour, and weapons. Professionals were engaged to manufacture the weapons and accoutrements for soldiers. It is likely that the artisans engaged in the production of military ware accompanied the army to the battlefield. In the Vedic age it was the responsibility of the state to provide clothes, weapons and armour to soldiers to enable them to fight the battle with vigour and without fear.[79]

NOTES

1. उत स्वयं तन्वः शुम्भमानाः । *Ṛgveda*, 7.56.11.
2. येषां श्रियाधि रोदसी विभ्राजन्ते रथेष्वा । Ibid., 5.61.12.
3. नैतावदन्ये मरुतो यथेमे भ्राजन्ते रुक्मैरायुधैस्तनूभिः । Ibid., 7.57.3.
4. Ibid., 1.166.10; *Atharvaveda*, 5.21.7.
5. Ibid., 5.52.9.
6. यमा इव सुसदृशः सुपेशसः । Ibid., 5.57.4.
7. *Vedic Index*, vol. 2, p. 292.
8. *Ṛgveda*, 1.26.1, 95.7, 115.4; 8.3.24.
9. Moti Chandra, *Prācīna Bhāratīya Veśa-bhūṣā*, p. 15.
10. *Ṛgveda*, 1.25.13; 9.86.14.
11. Ibid., 1.31.15.
12. *Vedic Index*, vol. 1, pp. 60-1; also see p. 383.
13. *Ṛgveda*, 1.166.10; *Atharvaveda*, 5.21.7; *Śatapatha Br.* 5.2.1.21, 24.
14. *Ṛgveda*, 6.75.1.
15. Ibid., 6.75.18.
16. E.W. Hopkins, *Position of the Ruling Caste in Ancient India*, p. 49.
17. *Atharvaveda*, 5.21.7; also *Ṛgveda*, 1.166.10.
18. जमूतस्येव भवति प्रतीकं यद्वर्मी याति समदामुपस्थे ।
    अनाविद्धया तन्वा जय त्वं स त्वा वर्मणो महिमा पिपर्तु ।। *Ṛgveda*, 6.75.1.
19. *Atharvaveda*, 5.21.7.

20. नमो विल्मिने कवचिने च नमो वर्मिने च। *Vājasaneyī Saṁhitā,* 16.35.
21. Ram Gopal, *India in Vedic Kalpasūtras*, p. 185.
22. नमो बिल्मिने च कवचिने च नमो वर्मिणे च वरूथिने च नमः श्रुताय च श्रुतसेनाय च दुन्दुभ्याय चाहनन्याय च।। *Yajurveda*, 16.35; also fn. 17 above.
23. A.C. Das, *Ṛgvedic Culture*, p. 220.
24. S.D. Singh, *Ancient Indian Warfare*, p. 97.
25. शिप्राः शीर्षन् हिरण्ययो शुभ्रा व्यंजत श्रिये। *Ṛgveda,* 8.7.25; also *Atharvaveda*, 5.21.7.
26. *Ṛgveda*, 4.37.4.
27. Ibid., 2.34.3.
28. Ibid., 10.96.4.
29. Ibid., 1.29.2; 6.44.14.
30. Das, op. cit., p. 220.
31. *Ṛgveda*, 6.75.14.
32. *Vedic Index*, vol. 1, pp. 388-9.
33. *Ṛgveda,* 10.18.9.
34. धन्वना या धन्वनाजिं जयेम धन्वना तीव्राः
    समदो जयेम। धनुः शत्रोरपकामं कृणोति
    धन्वना सर्वाः प्रदिशो जयेम। Ibid., 6.75.2.
35. *Vedic Index*, vol. 1, p. 82.
36. *Ṛgveda*, 6.75.11.
37. Ralph T.H. Griffith, *The Hymns of the Ṛgveda*, p. 331.
38. *Ṛgveda*, 6.75.15.
39. Das, op. cit., pp. 334-5.
40. इषुधिः सङ्का पृतनाश्च सर्वाः
    पृष्ठे निनद्धो जयति प्रसूतः। *Yajurveda*, 29.42.
    नि सर्वसेन इषुधीरसक्त। *Ṛgveda*, 1.33.3.
    इषुमन्तो निषङ्गिणः। Ibid., 5.57.2.
41. *Ṛgveda*, 6.75.5.
42. Ibid., 6.75.14.
43. हस्तेषु खादिश्च। Ibid., 1.168.3.
44. Das, op. cit., pp. 220-1.
45. *Atharvaveda*, 5.21.10.
46. पत्सु खादयो *Ṛgveda*, 5.54.11.
    Protective device for hand was called *khādi.* See n. 43 above.
47. *Śatapatha Br.,* 5.4.3.19.
48. Roshan Elkazi, *Ancient Indian Costume*, pp. 16-17.

49. गणं पिष्टं रुक्मेभिरञ्जिभिः। *Ṛgveda*, 5.56.1.
50. शुभयन्ते अञ्जिभिस्तनूषु शुभ्रा दधिरे विरुक्मतः। Ibid., 1.85.3.
 वक्षः सु रुक्मा। Ibid., 5.54.11; 1.166.10.
 भ्रजसा रुक्मवक्षसो। Ibid., 10.78.2.
51. शुभयन्ते अञ्जिभिस्तनूषु। Ibid., 1.85.3.
52. त्रिवरूथम्। Ibid., 6.46.9.
53. *Atharvaveda*, 5.21.7.
54. ये अञ्जिषु ये वाशीषु स्वभानवः। *Ṛgveda*, 5.53.4.
55. Das, op. cit., p. 335.
56. Ibid., p. 216.
57. Ram Gopal, op. cit., p. 185.
58. *Ṛgveda*, 7.85.2; 10.103.11; *Atharvaveda*, 5.21.12
59. Das, op. cit., p. 143.
60. अस्माकमिन्द्रः समृतेषु ध्वजेष्वस्माकं या इषवस्ता जयन्तु। *Ṛgveda*, 10.103.11.
61. स्पर्धन्ते वा उ देवहूये अत्र येषु ध्वजेषु दिद्यवः पतन्ति। Ibid., 7.85.2.
62. Ibid., 1.10.1.
63. एता देवसेनाः सूर्यकेतवः सचेतसः। *Atharvaveda*, 5.21.12.
64. Moti Chandra, op. cit., p. 23.
65. *Kātyāyana Śrauta-Sūtra*, 8.5.8.
66. *Śāṇḍilya Śrauta-Sūtra*, 8.6.12; also *Pañcaviṁśa Br.* 17.14-16; *Lāṭyāyana Śrauta-Sūtra*, 8.5.8; 8.6.12-13.
67. Singh, op. cit., pp. 23-5.
68. A.A. Macdonell, *A History of Sanskrit Literature*, p. 165; Dikshitar, however, holds that it carried only one person who functioned as warrior and charioteer both, to begin with. *War in Ancient India*, p. 158.
69. *Ṛgveda*, 10.39.14
70. *Atharvaveda*, 3.5.6
71. *Vedic Index*, vol. 2, p. 202, for full details, pp. 201-3.
72. *Ṛgveda*, 1.88.2.
73. हिरण्य चक्रान। Ibid., 1.88.5.
74. Macdonell, op. cit., p. 150; also *Vedic Index*, vol. 1, p. 42.
75. A.B. Keith, *Cambridge History of India*, vol. 1, p. 88.
76. P.C. Chakravarti, *The Art of War in Ancient India*, p. 33.
77. *Ṛgveda*, 5.61.1-3; A Vedic scholar has translated the terms *amīsavaḥ* (*Ṛgveda*, 5.61.2) and *aśvājani* (*Ṛgveda*, 6.75.13; *Yajurveda*, 29.50) as rein and whip respectively. For a detailed description see Das, op. cit., pp. 222-7.

78. अश्वैर्हिरण्यपाणिभिः। *Ṛgveda*, 8.7.27.
79. मर्माणि ते वर्मणा छादयामि सोमस्त्वा राजाभृतेनानु वस्ताम्।
उरोर्वरीयो वरुणस्ते कृणोतु जयन्तं त्वानु देवा मदन्तु।। *Ṛgveda*, 6.75. 18-19.

CHAPTER 5

Soldier in the Epics

CONCEPT OF UNIFORM

In the epics, soldiers have been described as puting on *saṅgrāmasajjā* (battle dress or military costume) before joining a battle,[1] and that it gave them a distinct look.[2] The Madra soldiers (of Punjab) appeared in the Kaurava camp dressed in attractive costume, mounting unique chariots and carrying unique weapons.[3] A thousand strong band of *rājaputras*, which opposed Abhimanyu in a battle, was uniformly dressed in red costume.[4] The security guards of Yudhiṣṭhira donned red garments and carried a sword.[5] Thus it appears that soldiers wore some kind of uniform before joining battle.[6] The kings and the commanders used fine drapery. Rāvaṇa's battle-dress was worked with gold and dyed in scarlet.[7] Bhīṣma was dressed in bright white garments (*śuklavāsasaḥ*)[8] and so were many other commanders.[9]

It appears that the state provided for the dress, weapons and equipment of soldiers. Heaps of weapons and armour were stored at the gates of the fort for the use of soldiers.[10] In fact, the state maintained large stores of weapons and accoutrements and various kinds of armour and equipment.[11]

But these allusions to costume and accoutrements do not present a complete picture of the Epic warrior. According to Vaidya:

there are hardly any references to the male costume in the epic. When Draupadi was brought in the assembly of princes it is stated that Duryodhana bared his right thigh in her sight. This could have been only possible with a *dhotī* worn in a manner not very different from today.... The second garment worn by males is very rarely mentioned. Presumably, an *uttarīya* was worn to cover the upper part of the body.[12]

Hopkins describes the Epic warrior as follows:

We saw ... the ready knight stand armed with bow and breastplate, and wear, besides, rings on his arms and in his ears. Another we saw wearing red, yellow, white and black clothes. The princes royal are arrayed in red. To these ornaments we must add the garlands with which each knight went into battle; the gems and diamonds worn about the armor, and even set in the common arms; the rings, again, worn upon the fingers; the chains of gold and pearl; the girdles of gold; and the tinkling bells of sword and club and chariot.... We have to add to all this adornment the fans (*vyajana*), the umbrella (*chattra*, spoken of above), and 'tails' or chowries (*cāmara*), which are in part insignia of royal office.[13]

COSTUME AND ACCOUTREMENTS

The descriptions of the battles in the epics, however, furnish useful details on military costume.

1. During a fierce battle between Droṇa and Abhimanyu the dress (*vastra*), ornaments (*ābharaṇa*), weapons (*śastra*), standards (*dhvaja*), armour (*varma*) and equipment (*āyudha*) of the warriors lay strewn on the battlefield. Swords (*khaḍga*), shields (*carman*), armours (*kavaca*), bows (*cāpa*) and heads also lay scattered.[14]
2. Abhimanyu covered the battlefield with bodies of his adversaries with their arms lopped off. Some arms were protected with gloves made of iguana skin; some held

bows and shafts; some grasped swords, or bucklers of iron, hooks, and rein; some held lances and axes; some clutched maces or iron balls or spears. Some had in their grasp scimitars or battle-axes; some held short darts, or shafts or *kampanas*; some held goads and big conch shells; some wielded piked lances and *kaca-grahas*; some had mallets or other kinds of missiles; some had nooses, heavy clubs and brick-bats. These arms were ornamented with bracelets and bangles and smeared with fragrant perfumes and unguents.[15]

3. After the death of Abhimanyu, the battlefield was seen littered with the heads of warriors adorned with ear-rings (*kuṇḍala*) and precious and variegated head-gears; and streamers and *cāmaras*, and splendid blankets; and gem-embossed weapons of good make, and the bright ornaments of cars and horses and men and elephants; and sharp and well tempered swords looking like snakes freed from their slough; and bows and shattered arrows, and darts and scimitars and spears and *kampanas* and various other kinds of weapons.[16]
4. In another context the battlefield is described as strewn with flag-staffs and car bottoms; with ornaments of cars, elephants and steeds; with shattered chariots, wheels, axels and *kuvaras*; with gold decked bows of fierce twang, and with thousands of arrows and darts furnished with wings of gold; with numerous lances, javelins, swords, and battle-axes; with maces and clubs and axes all adorned with gold; with standards of various descriptions and darts and piked bludgeons; and with beautiful *śataghnis*, the earth looked beautiful. Strewn all over again were ear-rings and necklaces of gold and fallen-off bracelets and rings and precious gems worn or diadems and crowns and turbans and golden ornaments of diverse kinds, and armours and leathern fences, and elephant-girths and umbrellas dropped from their place, and *cāmaras* and fans.[17]

5. At another place the battlefield is described as strewn with arrows, sharp weapons, broken vehicles of war, military equipment, armour, shields, necklaces, heads with ear-rings, turbans, crowns, garlands, clothing (*ambara*), neck-guards (*graiveya*), armlets (*aṅgada*), bright pendants (*niṣka*) and other ornaments. Broken chariot parts (*anukarṣa*, etc.) large quivers (*upāsaṅga*), flags, standards, adornments (*upaṣkara*), neck ropes (*kalapa*), various kinds of weapons, hunters (*kaśā*), bells (*ghaṇṭā*), howdahs (*bhāṇḍa*), garlands, ornaments and garments (*vastra*), were also scattered in the battlefield.[18]
6. Warriors donned skin garments.[19] The generals of the Kaurava army, viz., Śakuni, Śalya, Jayadratha, Vinda, Anuvinda, Kaikeya prince, Sudakṣiṇa, Śrutāyudha, Jayatsena, Bṛhadbala, and Kṛtavarmā, who commanded an *akṣauhiṇī* each, all dressed in a costume made of dear skin before joining the battle.[20]

Such references to military costume and accoutrements are abounding in the *Mahābhārata*. The information thus supplied by the Epic is almost sufficient to form a true picture of the warrior. The notable items of the dress and equipment of a warrior included the following:[21]

1. *Uṣṇīṣa* (headdress or turban)
2. *Vastra*, *vasana* or *uttarīya* (upper garment)
3. *Ambara* (lower garment or *dhotī*)
4. *Śirastrāṇa* (head-guard or helmet)
5. *Kavaca, varma, uracchada, ācchādana, paricchada, tanutrāṇa, tanucchada* (types of armour)
6. *Hastavāpa* (hand-guard)
7. *Aṅgulitrāṇa* (finger-guard)
8. *Keyūra* (bracelet)
9. *Aṅgada* (armlet)
10. *Graiveya* (neck-guard or necklace)
11. *Niṣka* (pendant)

12. *Kuṇḍala* (ear-ring)
13. *Paṭṭikam* (hair-band)
14. *Carma* (shield)
15. *Tuṇīra* (quiver)
16. *Śaṅkha* (conch)
17. *Saṁjñā* (identification mark)
18. Weapons (bow, sword, spear, etc.)

In the Epic Paraśurāma is portayed as a warrior donning an armour adorned with sun and moon symbols. He carried a bow in hand, hung a quiver on the back, and bore a finger-guard of skin.[22] This is perhaps the most specific reference to an Epic warrior. The rulers and senior commanders dressed in white garments (*śuklavāsasaḥ*) which included turban (*uṣṇīṣa*), lower garment (*antarīya*) and upper garment (*uttarīya*)[23] and wore armour (*varma*).[24]

In the Epic the terms *vasana*, *ambara*, and *vastra* generally convey the sense of garment or apparel, but which of these denoted upper garment or lower garment is not certain. Perhaps, the words, *vastra* and *vasana* denoted an *uttarīya* or upper garment as it was waived in the air by the warriors whenever there was occasion to rejoice at the battlefield.[25] The *ambara* may have denoted the lower garment as there is no reference to its waiving in the air. Warriors put on some kind of armour before joining the battle.

The state maintained huge stocks of weapons and accoutrements for use in war. These were indeed shifted to military camps (*skandhāvāra*) at the time of war. In the Pāṇḍava camp at Kurukṣetra large stocks of bow-strings (*pratyañcā*), bows, armours, weapons and eatables were maintained for the use of soldiers.[26]

As for the individual items of military costume it appears that the use of *uṣṇīṣa* (turban) was common among the soldiers.[27] It was perhaps used in combination with *śirastrāṇa* (head-protector or helmet) or without it.[28] Alternately, warriors used a hair-band to prevent the hair from obstructing the vision.[29] Excepting a solitary reference to *kañcuka* in relation to cavalrymen[30] there is no mention of stitched upper garment in the Epic. The *kavaca* and *varma* which were widely used by the soldiers in the Epic age perhaps served as armour and upper garment both. To cover the lower half of the body the soldiers used a *dhotī* like garment called *ambara*.[31] The use of ornaments like ear-rings, neck-chains, armlets, and garlands was common among soldiery.[32] Some kind of footwear was also in vogue.[33]

ŚAṄKHA AND *DHVAJA*

In the Epic age all warriors of repute carried a conch (*śaṅkha*) along with weapons. In the Epic war Śrīkṛṣṇa, Arjuna, Bhīma, Yudhiṣṭhira, Nakula and Sahadeva carried conches called *Pāñcajanya, Devadatta, Pauṇḍra, Anantavijaya, Sughoṣa* and *Maṇipuṣpaka* respectively.[34] Kaurava warriors also carried conches. Blowing of the conch signalled the commencement of hostilities.

The *dhvaja* was another important accoutrement. All senior warriors displayed a *dhvaja* on top of their chariot. Among the Pāṇḍavas and Kauravas, Arjuna chose a *vānara*, Yudhiṣṭhira a pair of *mṛdaṅgas*, Bhīma a *siṁha*, Duryodhana a *nāga*, Bhīṣma a *tāla*-tree, and Kṛpācārya a *vṛṣabha* as *dhvaja* emblem (*ketu*).[35]

LONG HAIR

Soldiers generally donned long hair, beard and moustache. In a combat they caught hold of each other's hair to pull down the adversary.[36] Occasionally, the head of the enemy was chopped by holding his hair by hand.[37] Heads of the dead soldiers with beard, moustache and long hair could be seen strewn in the battlefield.[38] When the Pāṇḍava army was severely punished by Bhīṣma, the soldiers ran away from the battlefield in dishevelled hair.[39] It was a general belief that people with long hair, beard and moustache were blessed with ideal progeny.[40]

But shaving was not totally unknown. It was believed that a person should shave either facing the east or the north as it ensured a long life.[41]

BODY ARMOUR

In the *Mahābhārata* the words *kavaca* and *varma* are widely used for defensive armour. The warriors invariably tied it to their body before joining a battle. During the *svayaṁvara* ceremony at the court of Kāśirāja the participant rulers put on *varma* to fight Bhīṣma.[42] While preparing to beat back the Kaurava raid the army commanders of Virāṭa put on *kavaca* or *varma.*[43] Even the Pāṇḍava brothers, who volunteered to help them in the battle were provided with armour.[44] The Pañcāla soldiers were equipped with *kavaca* when they came to join the Pāṇḍavas on the eve of the great war.[45]

Though *kavaca*[46] and *varma*[47] appear synonymous, their occurrence in some passages suggests that these were two different kinds of armour.[48] The *Amarakośa*, however, knew them as synonymous.[49]

Varma and *kavaca* were generally made of metals like copper, silver, and iron.[50] Perhaps, these were made of gold occasionally,[51] but there appears a lot of exaggeration in these references. The *kavaca* of Śatānīka, a brother of King Virāṭa, is said to have been made of gold and strengthened with diamond and iron inlays.[52] Another brother Madirākṣa used a *varma* made of iron and plated with gold.[53] The armour of Bhīṣma was made of black iron and was worked on with gold.[54] Bronze armour was also known.[55] In short, iron, copper, brass, silver, gold, wood and hide were used to make armour.[56] *Kavacas* are described as shining, suggesting that these were generally made of fine metal.[57] Quality armour was made by expert artisans (*śilpīvaraiḥ*) and its production consumed considerable time (*sudīrghakāla*).[58]

The armour was generally plated with gold and decorated with sacred motifs. The *kavaca* of King Virāṭa was marked by the symbols of one hundred suns, one hundred circles, one hundred dots, one hundred eyes and one hundred lotuses.[59] The *varma* of prince Śaṅkha was marked with one hundred symbols of eyes.[60] Nails were also planted on armour to make it strong.[61] Thus the armour was generally decorated with sun and moon symbols[62] and inlaid with gems and jewels.[63] It was tied to the body with the help of loops.[64]

Warriors went to sleep after putting off their armour.[65] Sometimes they vowed to put off their armour only after killing the enemy. Droṇa vowed to kill Pañcālas before he put off his *kavaca*.[66] Aśvatthāman also took a similar vow before joining battle against the Pañcālas.[67] Arjuna assured Kṛṣṇa that he would remove his armour only after killing Karṇa.[68]

Kavaca gave protection to the warrior in a great measure, but the skill lay in making it invulnerable. Droṇa had mastered this art and his armour could not be pierced through by any adversary.[69] On one occasion Droṇa tied *kavaca* on the body of Duryodhana in such a manner that no weapon could penetrate it.[70]

Occasionally, the term *tanucchada* (body cover) also occurs for armour. It was indeed the same as *kavaca*. In a fierce battle between Bhīma and Karṇa both suffered

Plate 3: Epic soldier

broken armour (*tanucchada*).[71] *Kavaca* was also called *tanutrāṇa* (protector of the body)[72] and it was not advisable to take it off.[73]

The armour could not, however, provide full protection to the warriors. In the *Mahābhārata* there are numerous references to arrows piercing through the armour.[74] While fleeing from the battlefield soldiers cast away their armour so as to gain speed.[75]

HELMET, ETC.

Helmet (*śirastrāṇa*) provided protection to the head. Duryodhana put on a helmet before joining the battle with Bhīma.[76] Babhruvāhana covered his head with helmet before engaging Arjuna in a battle.[77] Ghaṭotkaca also put on a helmet before going to battle.[78] Perhaps, helmet was tied to the head[79] with the turban (*uṣṇīṣa*).[80] It was either made of gold or plated with gold for senior commanders.[81]

However, the helmet provided limited protection as there are many references in the Epic to the severed heads of warriors in the battlefield. Sahadeva chopped the head of Duḥśāsana's charioteer along with his *śirastrāṇa*.[82] Kṛpācārya and Śrutakarman also severed the heads of their adversaries protected by helmets, in the battle.[83] At the end of the day the battlefield could be seen littered with helmets of dead soldiers.[84] Neck was protected by *kaṇṭhatrāṇa*.[85]

Palm-guard (*talatra*) was a leathern fence worn by archers on the left hand while joining a battle.[86] When struck by the bow-string it made a sound with reverberation.[87]

Aṅgulitrāṇa was a contrivance used by archers to protect fingers from injury while pulling the bow-string. Generally made of iguana skin,[88] it was tied to the hand while going to battle.[89]

Hastavāpa was again a kind of cover used by archers to protect hands. An archer targetted the *hastavāpa* of his adversary so as to deprive him of the protection.[90] When struck by the bow-string it made a sound in the battlefield.[91] It seems that *hastavāpa aṅgulitrāṇa* and *talatrāṇa* protected the archer's hand from injury by his own bow string. All warriors carried an identification mark on their person.[92]

Legs were protected by shoes, but there are few references to it in the *Mahābārata*,[93] suggesting that it was not a common wear.

SHIELD

Shield (*carman*), generally made of ox-hide, was the most common defensive weapon, particularly for the infantry soldier.[94] Charioteers also carried it for use in emergency.[95] Shields were generally decorated with gold nets, gold covers, and crescent and star symbols.[96] *Śarāvara* and *phalaka*, perhaps made of material other than *carma*, are the other shield types mentioned in the Epics.[97]

WEAPONS

The bow, variously called *dhanuṣ*, *cāpa*, *śarāsana*, *kārmuka*, and *śāraṅga*, was the principal weapon of the Epic warrior. It was generally made of *kārmuka* wood[98] but the bow made of horn was considered the best.[99] A cane-bow may also have been common among the soldiers. The length of the bow is occasionally said to be *tāla-mātra* (as big as a palm),[100] but both long and short bows were known.[101] The string of the bow (*jyā*) was made of *mūrvā*-grass, multiple strands bound together in one. It was dried hard and when pressed against the hand-guard produced a sound.[102] Its repeated contact with the body left a permanent mark on the arm of bowman.[103]

The bows were generally decorated. The oft-repeated expression 'bow with a golden back' seems to suggest that some kind of gilding or ornamentation was common.[104] A bow has been described as adorned with the figures of five leopards.[105]

The arrow was variously called as *iṣu*, *śara*, *śalya*, *bhalla*, *pradara*, *nārāca*, etc. It was generally made of reed (*vainava*) or iron (*ayasa*). Arrows of bone were also known. Arrow comprised a blade (*śalya*), a shaft (*nālikā*), and some feathers (*paṅkha*). The blade was fastened to the shaft with sinews.[106] Feathers of flamingos and herons attached to the lower end of the shaft gave arrow the desired speed and balance. The feathers of hawk[107] and vulture[108] were also used, occasionally. The crescent-head (*ardha-candra*) and calf's-tooth (*vatsadanta*) types of arrows were most popular.[109] The other types mentioned in the Epic include *nārāca*, *nālikā*, *varāhakarṇa*, *bhalla*, *añjalika* and *kṣurapra*.[110] The less respected category of arrows included goat-horn arrows, needle-shaped arrows, rotten arrows, crooked arrows, poisoned arrows, and the arrows made with monkey, cow or elephant bones.[111] The normal length of an arrow is said to have been equal to the axle of a war car, which Egerton is inclined to put between two and a half feet to three feet.[112]

Quiver, variously called *iṣudhi*, *tūṇa*, *tūṇīra*, *niṣaṅga*, *upāsaṅga* and *kalapa*, also formed a part of soldier's accoutrement. Of these *niṣaṅga* and *tūṇīra* types were used by foot-soldiers. *Upāsaṅga* was carried by warriors mounted on chariot, elephant or horse. The *tūṇa* was used by charioteers.[113] Foot-soldiers carried two large quivers (*niṣaṅga*) on the right back.[114] A quiver generally carried ten to twenty arrows.[115]

Next to the bow, the club called *gadā* or *mausala* was the most popular weapon of the Epic warrior. Warriors like Balarāma, Bhīma, Śalya, and Duryodhana had specialized in the use of this weapon. It was made of iron or wood, bore six to eight edges and was sharp and gold plated.[116]

The sword, known as *asi*, *khaḍga* and *nistriṁsa* in the epics, was another important weapon.[117] It was kept in a sheath (*kośa*) made of tiger skin, and was unsheathed only during a battle.[118] Some warriors carried a sword provided with ivory hilt and worked with gold.[119] Sword was adorned with ornaments[120] and its sheath was decorated with small bells.[121]

The spear or javelin (*śakti*) was another important weapon. It was made of iron and decorated with gold plating or gilding and with beryl.[122] The Epic mentions many more weapons of offensive and defensive nature as also firearms and divine weapons.

VEHICLES OF WAR

Chariot

The chariot is described as two-wheeled, four-wheeled or even eight-wheeled vehicle drawn by two, four, or eight horses respectively. One or more charioteers were employed to drive it, depending on the number of horses drawing it.[123] A whip was used to control and command the horses.

The chariot comprised an axle, to which the wheels were attached. Above the axle was the seat of the charioteer, while a little behind was the place of the knight. The box of the chariot (*rathonīḍa*) was firmly fixed to the axle. The wheel consisted, besides the wooden circle of the tyre (*rathanemi*), the spokes (*āra*) and the hub (*nābhi*). *Varūtha* was perhaps the railing or protective screen of the knight. The pole of the car (*ratha-īsā*) was fastened to the box of the car (*kāṣṭha*) and the double yoke (*yuga*) rested on the neck of the horses. The fastenings of the yoke were termed *yoktra* or *saṁnahana*. These as well as the reins appear to have been made of leather. Attached to the chariot was a pole (*yaṣṭi*) on which the warrior's standard (*dhvaja*) was displayed.[124]

In the Epics the chariots are described as upholstered with the skin of tiger or some other animal. Rāma mounted a *vaiyāghra* chariot on the eve of his consecration as *yuvarāja*.[125] At the time of the *Rājasūya* sacrifice the rulers of eastern countries presented Yudhiṣṭhira with *vaiyāghra* chariots.[126] The army of Duryodhana included chariots covered with the skins of tigers and elephants.[127] Chariots were also covered with the skin of the bear.[128] The following extracts from the epics help in forming a complete picture of war chariot.

1. The chariot was well tied up with ropes, provided with standards and flags, decorated with small bells and carried sword, shield and *paṭṭisa* (a weapon). Each chariot was drawn by four horses of fine pedigree and carried spears and staff (*ṛṣṭika*) and one hundred arrows. Two horses were managed by one charioteer.[129]
2. The eight-wheeled car of Ghaṭotkaca was made of iron and was large and awful. It was covered with bear skin, equipped with weapons and armours, and adorned with garlands.[130]
3. Rāvaṇa mounted his divine car drawn by black horses, furnished with all kinds of weapons, sounding with a hundred bells, harnessed with tough swift steeds, and well guided by the charioteer; which had the sound of thunder, and the glory of the shining moon or sun; which had a lofty flag staff which was irresistible, furnished with a protection, well adorned, covered with a net of gold, on fire as it were with glory.[131]
4. The chariot of Droṇācārya was provided with armour of tiger-skin (*vaiyāghra parivāritam*).[132] Perhaps, such adornments were exclusive to the chariots of high

ranking commanders.[133] These descriptions in the epics suggest that the chariot ensemble comprised the following:

1. Rows of bells
2. Coverings of tiger skin
3. Golden net
4. Store for weapons
5. Lofty *dhvaja* staff
6. Ornamented doors
7. Two to eight horses
8. Two to eight wheels
9. One to four charioteers, depending on the number of horses.
10. *Pratoḍa* (whip like device carried by charioteers)

Elephant

In the Epic war the elephant played a subordinate role to the chariot. In fact, 'the greater chiefs, princes, kings, mount elephants so rarely that we may be entitled to infer that the practice of a king fighting from a great howdah (*vimāna*) on an elephant's back is later than the other methods of car-fighting, and that mention of it will be among the later additions'.[134] However, an elephant when deployed in battlefield carried as many as seven riders, viz., two goadsters, two archers, two swordsmen, and one trident or spear bearer.[135]

Elephants were equipped with some kind of armour before being led to battle.[136] Generally, thorny armour or iron armour protected the elephants.[137] Perhaps, armour made of iron or black iron was considered durable.[138] Occasionally, the armour was made of cow, ox or python hide.[139] Powerful arrow-shots could, however, pierce through the elephant armour. Arjuna is said to have destroyed the armour of Bhāgdatta's elephant in an encounter.[140] Abhimanyu also destroyed the armour of many elephants in an encounter with Kauravas.[141] In the *Mahābhārata* the battlefield is described as full of dead elephants with shattered armour.[142]

The covering laid on the back of the elephant was made of wool[143] and was called *kaṁbala, āstara, rāṅkava, āstaraṇa*, etc. *Kutha*, a coloured woollen blanket, was a common spread.[144]

The *vimāna* (howdah) placed on the elephant back was made in various designs. An elephant provided with *padmavimāna*, i.e. an eight-pillared and eight-cornered saddle, was called *padmina*.[145]

The *aṅkuśa* (goad) and *tottra* (whip) were used to command the animal.[146] Though assumed to be synonymous in the Epic, these are mentioned as different implements,[147] perhaps meant to serve different purposes. In the Epics the equipment of the elephant includes the following:[148]

1. *Vaijayanta* (flag)
2. *Aṅkuśa* (goad)
3. *Dhvaja* (standard)
4. *Tūṇa* (quiver)
5. *Varma, tanutra* (armour)
6. *Kakṣya* (girth)
7. *Graiveya* (neck-guard)
8. *Kaṁbala* (back-spread)
9. *Ghaṇṭā* (bell)
10. *Chatra* (parasol)
11. *Mālā* (garland)
12. *Tottra* (hunter)
13. *Vimāna* (howdah)
14. *Danta-veṣṭaiḥ* (adornments of teeth)
15. *Bhāṇḍa* (trappings)

HORSE

In the Epics cavalry appears as an important arm. However, its role seems to have been subordinate to that of the chariot and the elephant corps as stated by Hopkins:

> the mounted soldiers are recognized as a body (*kulam*) apart from others, of course, but do not act together. They appear as concomitants of the war-cars, dependent groups; but separate horsemen appear everywhere. Their employment was much influenced by that of the elephants. A body of horsemen is routed by an elephant. They were, therefore, detailed in small numbers to guard the war-cars and keep on the flanks of their own elephants. To the latter, indeed, they are formally assigned, but seem generally to be circling about the chariots.[149]

Horses were also provided with some kind of armour. In the Epics there are many references to *ūrucchada* (breast-plate) of the horse.[150] Horse armour was also called *kavaca.*[151] Occasionally, horses were covered with tiger skin.[152] The horse armour was decorated with golden nets, gems and moon symbols in gold.[153]

The seat on the horse-back was called *pīṭhaka, paristoma pīṭhamarda, āstaraṇa,* etc.[154] It was made of *rāṅkava* or *kaṁbala.*[155] The bit (*khalina*) was known and in the Epic the battlefield is described as littered with *khalinas* of the horses, who had lost their riders.[156] The horse was driven by a whip (*kaśā*), unlike an elephant which was driven by a goad.[157] The whip was tied to the wrist of the rider to allow free use of the hand.[158] In the Epics the main equipment of the horse comprised the following.[159]

1. *Carmakavaca* (skin-armour)
2. *Camara* (yak-tail)
3. *Chanaghaṇṭāna* (garland of bells)
4. *Kakṣya* (girth)
5. *Pīṭhaka* (seat on the back)

6. *Khalina* (bit)
7. *Tūṇīra* (quiver)
8. *Raśmi* (bridle)
9. *Bhāṇḍa* (trappings)
10. *Kaśā* (whip)

The concept of military uniform or battle-dress thus appears in a evolved stage in the Epics. The occurrence of the term *saṅgrāmasajjā* (battle-dress) in the *Rāmāyaṇa* confirms this. The warriors generally dressed in *uṣṇīṣa* (turban), *vastra* or *uttarīya* (upper garment) and *ambara* or *vasana* (lower garment). The use of stitched garments had not yet become common. Soldiers used some kind of armour to protect the body. Boots had not become a part of military uniform. Chariots, elephants, and horses were also provided with some kind of protective armour.

Foot-soldiers generally fought with shields, swords and spears. The principal weapon of the chariot warriors was bow. Cavalrymen used sword and shield, but spear was their favourite weapon. Elephant riders fought with spear and carried a shield for protection.

NOTES

1. संग्रामसज्जाः संहृष्टा धारयन् राक्षसास्तदा।
   राधनुष्काः कवचिनो वेगादाप्लुत्य राक्षसाः।। *Rāmāyaṇa* (*Rām*), Yuddha, 57.23.
2. सैन्यैरद्भुतदर्शनैः। Ibid., 33.23.
3. विचित्रकवचाः शूरा विचित्रध्वजकार्मुकाः।
   विचित्राभरणाः सर्वे विचित्ररथवाहनाः।।
   स्वदेशवेषाभरणा वीराः शतसहस्रशः।
   तस्य सेना प्रणेतारो बभूवुः क्षत्रियर्षभाः।। *Mahābhārata* (*Mbh*), Udyoga, 8.3-4.
4. कृताभिसमयाः सर्वे सुवर्णविकृतध्वजाः।।
   रक्ताम्बरधराः सर्वे सर्वे रक्तविभूषणाः।
   सर्वेरक्तपताकाश्च सर्वे वै हेममालिनः।। Ibid., Droṇa, 33.13-14.

5. कच्चिद्रक्ताम्बरधराः खड्गहस्तास्वलंकृताः। Ibid., Sabhā, 5.77.
6. दत्तायुद्धपरिच्छदम्। Ibid., Vana, 16.21.
7. हेमसंच्छादिताम्बरम्। *Rām*, Yuddha, 40.5.
8. आप्लाव्य शुचयः सर्वे स्रग्विणः शुक्लवाससः। *Mbh.*, Udyoga, 196.2.
9. Ibid.
10. ददर्शायुधजालानि तथैव कवचानि च। *Rām,* Yuddha, 41.38.
11. नानाविकृतसंस्थानं वाजिभाण्डपरिच्छदम्।
गजग्रैवेयकक्ष्याश्च रथभाण्डांश्च संस्कृतान्।।
तनुत्राणि च योधानां हस्त्यश्वानां च वर्म च।
खड्गा धनूंषि ज्याबाणास्तोमराङ्कुशशक्तयः।। Ibid., 75.10-11.
12. C.V. Vaidya, *Epic India*, vol. 1, p. 141.
13. E.W. Hopkins, *Social and Military Position of the Ruling Caste in Ancient India*, pp. 261-2.
14. पुण्डरीकवनानीव विध्वस्तानि समन्ततः।
चक्राते द्रोणपाञ्चाल्यौ नृणां शीर्षाण्यनेकशः।।
विनिकीर्णानि वीराणामनीकेषु समन्ततः।
वस्त्राभरणशस्त्राणि ध्वजवर्मायुधानि च।। *Mbh*, Droṇa, 72.7-8; also Bhīṣma, 50.48-55; 51.28-32; 85.33-34; 102.20-22
15. वद्धगोधाङ्गुलित्राणान्सशरावरकार्मुकान्।
सासिचर्माङ्कुशाभीशून्सतोमरपरश्वधान् ।।
सगुडायोमुखप्रासान्सर्ष्टितोमरपट्टिशान् ।
सभिण्डिपालपरिघान्सशक्तिवरकम्पनान् ।।
सप्रतोदमहाशङ्खान्सकुन्तान्सकचग्रहान् ।
समुद्गरक्षेपणीयान्सपाशपरिघोपलान् ।।
सकेयूराङ्गदान्बाहून्हृद्यगन्धानुलेपनान् ।
संचिच्छेदार्जुनिर्वृत्तांस्त्वदीयानां सहस्रशः ।। Ibid., 35.23-26.
16. रुक्मपुङ्खैश्च संपूर्णा रुधिरौधपरिप्लुता ।
उत्तमाङ्गैश्च वीराणां भ्राजमानैः सकुण्डलैः ।।
विचित्रैश्च परिस्तोमैः पताकाभिश्च संवृता ।
चामरैश्च कुथाभिश्च प्रविद्धैश्चाम्बरोत्तमैः ।।
चापैश्च विशिखैश्छिन्नैः शक्त्यृष्टिप्रासकम्पनैः ।
विविधैरायुधैश्चान्यैः संवृताः भूरशोभत ।। Ibid., 48.23-26.
17. सानुकर्षपताकैश्च द्विपाश्वरथभूषणैः ।
स्यन्दनैरपविद्धैश्च भग्नचक्राक्षकूबरैः ।।
जातरूपपरिष्कारैर्धनुर्भिः सुमहाधनैः ।
सुवर्णपुङ्खैरिषुभिर्नाराचैश्च सहस्रशः ।।
कर्णपाण्डविनिर्मुक्तैनिर्मुक्तैरिव पन्नगैः ।

प्रासतोमरसंधातैः खड्गैश्च सपरश्वधैः ।।
सुवर्णविकृतैश्चापि गदामूसलपट्टिशेः ।
वज्रैश्च विविधाकारैः शक्तिभिः परिघैरपि।
शतघ्नीभिश्च चित्राभिर्बभौ भारत मेदिनी ।।
कनकाङ्गदकेयूरैः कुण्डलैर्मणिभिः शुभैः ।
तनुत्रैः सतलत्रैश्च हारैर्निष्कैश्च भारत ।।
वस्त्रैश्छत्रैश्च विध्वस्तैश्चामरव्यजनैरपि ।
गजाश्वमनुजैर्भिन्नैः शस्त्रैः स्यन्दनभूषणैः ।। Ibid., 113.17-22; also 48.43-45.

18. विकीर्णशस्त्राभरणा विपन्नाश्वरथद्विपाः ।
संछिन्नभिन्नवर्माणो वैक्लव्यं परमं गताः ।।
ससत्त्वा गतसत्त्वाश्च प्रभया परया युताः ।
सजीवा इव लक्ष्यन्ते गतसत्वा नराधिपाः ।।
तेषां शरैः स्वर्णपुङ्खैः शस्त्रैश्च विविधैः शितैः ।
वाहनैरायुधैश्चैव संपूर्णां पश्य मेदनीम् ।।
वर्मभिश्चर्मभिहरैः शिरोभिश्च सकुण्डलैः ।
उष्णीसैर्मुकुटैः स्रग्भिश्चूडामणिभिरम्बरैः ।।
कण्ठसूत्रैरङ्गदैश्च निष्कैरपि च सुप्रभैः ।
अन्यैश्चाभरणैश्चित्रैर्भाति भारत मेदनी ।।
चामरैर्व्यजनैश्चित्रैर्ध्वजैश्चाश्वरथद्विपैः ।
विविधैश्च परिस्तोमैरश्वानां च प्रकीर्णकैः ।।
कुथाभिश्च विचित्राभिर्वरूथैश्च महाधनैः ।
संस्तीर्णां वसुधां पश्य चित्रपटैरिवावृताम् ।। Ibid., 123.32-38

19. चीरसंवृतगात्राश्च तथा फलकवाससः ।
नानावेषधराश्चैव चर्मवासस एव च ।। Ibid., Śalya, 44.88.

20. संनद्धाः समदृश्यन्त स्वेष्वनीकेष्ववस्थिताः ।
वद्धकृष्णाजिना सर्वे ध्वजिनो मुञ्जमालिनः ।। Ibid., Bhīṣma, 16.37.

21. अभिज्ञानानि सर्वेषां संज्ञाश्चाभरणानि च । Ibid., 1.12.

22. ध्वजेन च महाबाहो सोमालंकृतलक्ष्मणा ।
धनुर्धरो वद्धतूणो वद्धगोधाङ्गुलित्रवान् ।। Ibid., Udyoga, 180.8;
In the Bombay Edition the word कवचेन is used in the place of ध्वजेन।

23. शुक्लवासाः सितोष्णीषः सर्वशुक्लविभूषणः । Ibid., 179.14.
उष्णीषाणि नियच्छन्तः पुण्डरीकनिभैः करैः ।
अन्तरीयोत्तरीयाणि भूषणानि च सर्वशः ।। Ibid., Udyoga, 150.20.

24. दंशितः पाण्डुरेणाहं कवचेन वपुष्मता । Ibid., 179.12.

25. वस्त्राणि दुधुवुश्च ह । Ibid., Droṇa, 20.8; 84.25; Karṇa, 89.9 (BE).
26. ज्याधनुवर्मशस्त्राणां तथैव मधुसर्पिषोः ।
ससर्जरसपांसूनां राशयः पर्वतोपमः ।। Ibid., Udyoga, 152.13; also 152.14-15 (BE).
27. सोष्णीषं सशिरस्त्राणं क्षुरप्रेणान्वपातयत् । Ibid., Karṇa, 38.28; *uṣṇīṣa* is widely mentioned in the epics.
28. Ibid., 38.28.
29. समुद्ग्रथ्य सितेन वाससा । Ibid., 66.19
केशान समनुमृज्य च । Ibid., Sabhā, 21.6.
30. हययोधानपश्याम कञ्चुकोष्णीषधारिणः । Ibid., Karṇa, 17.109.
31. विशीर्णवर्माभरणाम्बरायुधैः । Ibid., 68.19.
32. Ibid., 123.32-38; *Rām*, Yuddha, 53.6; 57.22; 65.25-29.
33. *Mbh.*, Bhīṣma, 102.22; Karṇa 58.22 (BE); Karṇa, 8.19. In *Mbh* there is a reference to god Sūrya offering चर्मपादुक to sage Jāmdagnya. Anuśāsana, 96.14 (BE).
34. पाञ्चजन्यं हृषीकेशो देवदत्तं धनंजयः ।
पौण्ड्रं दध्मौ महाशङ्खं भीमकर्मा वृकोदरः ।।
अनन्तविजयं राजा कुन्तीपुत्रो युधिष्ठिरः ।
नकुलः सहदेवश्च सुघोषमणिपुष्पकौ ।। *Mbh*, Bhīṣma, 23.15-16.
35. For details see U.P. Thapliyal, *The Dhvaja*, pp. 55-6.
36. कचाकचि वभौ युद्धम् । *Mbh*, Karṇa, 33.60.
आसीत्केशपरामर्शो मुष्टियुद्धं च दारुणम् । Ibid., Droṇa, 31.26.
मारुतोद्धूतकेशान्तम् । Ibid., 48.2
मुक्तकेशाः । Ibid., 146.92 (BE)
37. केशपक्षे परामृश्य जहार समरे शिरः । Ibid., Bhīṣma, 57.14 (BE).
38. क्लृप्तश्मश्रुभिरत्यर्थं । Ibid., Karṇa, 14.50
ताड्यमानाः क्षितिं जग्मुर्मुक्तकेशाः शरार्दिताः । *Mbh*, Droṇa, 32.48 (BE).
39. प्रकीर्य केशान् धावन्तः प्रत्यदृश्यन्त भारत । Ibid., Bhīṣma, 102.28; also Sauptika, 8.90.
40. केशश्मश्रूधारयतामग्र्या भवति संततिः । Ibid., Anuśāsana, 57.23.
41. प्राङ्मुखः श्मश्रुकर्माणि कारयेत समाहितः ।
उदङ्मुखो वा राजेन्द्र तथायुर्विन्दते महत् ।। Ibid., 107.121.
42. आमुञ्चतां च वर्माणि । *Mbh*, Ādi, 96.15.
43. Ibid., Virāṭa, 30.9-15; also Droṇa, 162.42; Śalya, 7.1.
44. Ibid., Virāṭa, 30.22, 26.
45. उपयात्सर्वसैन्यानां प्रतिच्छाद्य तदा वपुः । Ibid., Udyoga, 56.5.

46. बिभेद कवचं । Ibid., Karṇa, 33.28.
47. तद्वर्म हेमविकृतम् । Ibid., 33.29.
48. विध्वस्तचर्मकवचं । Ibid., Karṇa, 33.69.
49. In the *Amarakośa* (2.8.64) तनुय, वर्म, दंशन, कंकटक, जगर and कवच have been called synonymous.
50. ताम्रराजतलोहानां । *Mbh*, Virāṭa, 57.7.
51. स कांचनविचित्रेण कवचेन समावृतः । Ibid., Droṇa, 65.6.
    शुभकांचनवर्मभृत । Ibid., Śalya, 31.55.
    संनह्य कांचनं वर्म । Ibid., Āśvamedhika, 78.14.
    कवचैश्च हिरण्मयैः । Ibid., Droṇa, 73.25.
    ते वर्म हेमविकृतं भित्त्वा । Ibid., Karṇa, 42.9.
52. सवज्रायसगर्भं तु कवचं तप्तकाञ्चनम् । Ibid., Virāṭa, 30.10.
53. सर्वपारसवं वर्म । Ibid., 30.11.
54. तस्य कार्ष्णायसं वर्म हेमचित्रं महर्द्धिमत् । Ibid., Droṇa, 102.55.
55. कांसे निर्भिद्य वर्मणी। Ibid., 150.24.
56. E.W. Hopkins, *Position of the Ruling Caste in Ancient India*, p. 248.
57. वर्मणां तत्र राजेन्द्र व्यदृश्यन्तोज्ज्वलाः प्रभाः । *Mbh*, Śalya, 21.43; Droṇa, 70.26.
58. Ibid., Karṇa, 66.33.
59. शतसूर्यं शतावर्तं शतबिन्दु शताक्षिमत् ।
    अभेद्यकल्पं मत्स्यानां राजा कवचमाहरत् ।।
    उत्सेधे यस्य पद्मानि शतं सौगन्धिकानि च । Ibid., Virāṭa, 30.12-13.
60. श्वेतं वर्म शताक्षिमत् । Ibid., 30.14.
61. सकील कवचाः । Ibid., Udyoga, 155.8 (BE).
62. कवचेन महावाहो सोमार्ककृतलक्ष्मणा । Ibid., 179.8 (BE).
63. हैमं शुभ्रं मणिरत्नावभासि । Ibid., Droṇa, 2.23.
64. निवध्यतां मे कवचं । Ibid.
    द्रोणेनाबद्धकवचो । Ibid., 76.37
    न संधिः शक्यते भेत्तुं वर्मबन्धस्य तस्य तु । Ibid., 69.64.
65. विमुक्तयुग्यकवचा। Ibid., Sauptika, 3.25, Also 4.2.
66. नाहत्वा सर्वपाञ्चालान् कवचस्य विमोक्षणम् । Ibid., Droṇa, 126.32.
67. Ibid., Śalya, 29.21.
68. सत्यं वदाम्यद्य न कर्णमाजौ
    शरैरहत्वा कवचं विमोक्ष्ये ।। Ibid., Karṇa, 70.37 (BE).
69. अभेद्यकवचावृतः । Ibid., Droṇa, 86.24.

70. एष ते कवचं राजंस्तथा बध्नामि काञ्चनम् ।
यथा न बाणा नास्त्राणि विषहिष्यन्ति ते रणे ।। Ibid., 69.35.
द्रोणेनाबद्धकवचो राजा दुर्योधनस्तदा। Ibid., 76.37.
71. शरैश्छिन्नतनुच्छदौ। Ibid., 143.17; 111.23.
72. तस्य भित्वा तनुत्राणं भित्वा कायं च सायकः । Ibid., Karṇa, 51.37 (BE).
संनह्यतां तनुत्राणि । Ibid., Śānti, 4.15.
73. न जह्याच तनुत्राणं । Ibid., 120.13.
74. Ibid., Virāṭa, 57.4, 7.
ते वर्म भित्त्वा सुदृढं । Ibid., Droṇa, 85.6.
प्रविद्धवर्माभरणावरायुधा । Ibid., 48.46; also Bhīṣma, 108.26; Karṇa, 33.28-30.
75. विमुच्य कवचानन्ये पाण्डुपुत्रस्य सैनिकाः । Ibid., Bhīṣma, 102.28.
76. आवद्ध शिरस्त्राणः । Ibid., Śalya, 54.15.
77. Ibid., Aśvamedha, 78.14.
78. Ibid., Droṇa, 150.3.
79. आवद्ध । Ibid., Śalya, 54.15.
80. सोष्णीषं सशिरस्त्राणं क्षुरप्रेणान्वपातयत् । Ibid., Karṇa, 38.28.
81. रुक्माङ्गदशिरस्त्राणो । Ibid., Droṇa, 96.4.
जातरूपसशिरस्त्राणं । Ibid., 9.8 (BE).
82. माद्रीपुत्रः शिरो यन्तुः सशिरस्त्राणमच्छिनत् । Ibid., 188.2 (BE).
83. जहार सशिरस्त्राणं शिरस्तस्य महात्मनः । Ibid., Karṇa; 10.13, also 38.28.
84. दस्यूनां सशिरस्त्राणैः शिरोभिर्लूनमूर्धजैः । Ibid., Droṇa, 95.40.
85. कण्ठत्राणेन च बभौ सेन्द्रायुध इवाम्बुदः । Ibid., 102.56.
86. Ibid., Karṇa, 5.83.
87. ज्यातलत्रेषुशब्दांश्च । Ibid., 31.48.
88. बद्धगोधाङ्गुलित्राणः । Ibid., Ādi, 125.8, Droṇa, 35.23; Udyoga, 180.8; also Āśvamedhika, 72.8; Droṇa, 40.16; 43.14; Karṇa, 14.40.
89. Ibid.
90. हस्तवापं निकृत्य च । Ibid., Droṇa, 140.28, also 96.34, 137.28; Śalya, 9.32; Droṇa, 17.19, 78.28, 145.42; Virāṭa, 50.17.
91. Ibid., Karṇa, 16.21, Bhīṣma, 43.4.
92. अभिज्ञानानि सर्वेषां संज्ञाश्चाभरणानि च । Ibid., Bhīṣma, 1.12
93. Yudhiṣṭhira put on shoes (*upānaha*) at the time of coronation. Ibid., Sabhā, 49.8.
94. सचर्मणः पदातीनाम् । Ibid., Droṇa, 146.17 (BE)
आर्षभाणि विचित्राणि रुक्मजालवृतानि च ।

संपेतुर्दिक्षु सर्वासु चर्माणि भरतर्षभ ।। Ibid., Bhīṣma, 67.28; also *Rām*, Yuddha, 54.30.

95. Ibid., Bhīṣma, 49.34.
96. आर्षभे चर्मणी चित्रे शतचन्द्रपरिष्कृते ।
तारकाशतचित्रौ च निस्त्रिंशौ सुमहाप्रभौ ।। Ibid., 112.19; also 50.25; Droṇa, 91.40; Karṇa, 9.27, 30; *Rām,* Ayodhyā, 99.22.
97. Ibid., Bhīṣma, 56.17; 86.36; Droṇa, 13.50.
98. Ibid., Virāṭa, 38.46, 59.2, 59.24-25.
99. Ibid., Karṇa, 79.23 (BE).
100. तालमात्रम् धनुर्गृह्य । Ibid., Bhīṣma, 45.47.
101. वासवाशनिनिर्घोषं दृढज्यमभिविक्षिपन् ।
व्यक्तं किष्कुपरीणाहं द्वादशारत्नि कार्मुकम् ।। Ibid., Droṇa, 150.16.
102. वर्मदेहासुमथनैर्धनुषः प्रच्युतैः शरैः ।
मौर्व्या तलत्रैर्न्यवधीत्कशया वाजिनो यथा ।। Ibid., Karṇa, 16.21.
103. Ibid., Bhīṣma, 96.13.
104. रुक्मपृष्ठं महावेगं रुक्मचन्द्रकसंकुलम् । *Mbh*, Droṇa, 96.3; also Bhīṣma, 96.12; Virāṭa, 38.20-24.
105. पञ्चशार्दूललक्षणः । Ibid., Virāṭa, 38.50.
106. ते तु नामाङ्किताः पीताः कालज्वलनसंनिभाः ।
स्नायुनद्धाः सुपर्वाणः पृथवो दीर्घगामिनः ।। Ibid, Droṇa, 74.7.
107. Ibid., Virāṭa, 38.26.
108. Ibid., Droṇa, 95.34.
109. Ibid., Bhīṣma, 88.30; 90.2; Droṇa, 20.16, 91.23.
110. Ibid., Droṇa, 91.23; *Añjalika* was an important arrow type which was used by Arjuna to sever the head of Karṇa. *Mbh*, Karṇa, 67.16.
111. Ibid., Droṇa, 164.11-12.
112. *Indian Antiquary*, 1886, pp. 24-7.
113. Hopkins, op. cit., p. 220 fn.
114. अक्षय्यौ च महेषुधी। *Mbh*, Śalya, 61.9; also Ādi, 216.19; Udyoga, 59.12.
115. Hopkins, op. cit., p. 218.
116. *Mbh*, Śalya, 31.37; for details Hopkins, op. cit., p. 218.
117. Ibid., Droṇa, 164.135.
118. द्वीपिचर्मावनद्धैश्च व्याघ्रचर्मशतैरपि।
विकोशैर्विमलैः खड्गैरभिजघ्नुः परान्रणे।। *Mbh*, Bhīṣma, 44.32; Droṇa, 117.53; Virāṭa, 38.55.
119. हस्तिदन्तत्सरून्खड्गाञ्जातरूपपरिष्कृतान् । Ibid., Bhīṣma, 92.49; also Sabhā, 47.14; Karṇa, 56.37.

120. Ibid., Virāṭa, 38.50-58.
121. किङ्कणीजालसंछन्नं चर्मणा च परिष्कृतम् । *Rām*, Yuddha, 54.30; *Mbh*, Virāṭa, 38.32-33.
122. शक्त्यृष्टयः काञ्चनभूषिताश्च । *Mbh.*, Ādi, 186.7; Bhīṣma, 107.11, 49.14, 50.
123. For details on the equipment of horse see Hopkins, op. cit., pp. 179-84.
124. Ibid.
125. *Rām*, Ayodhyā, 16.28.
126. वैयाघ्रपरिवारणान् । *Mbh*, Sabhā, 47.29; also Droṇa, 8.8.
127. व्याघ्रचर्म परीवारा वृताश्च द्वीपिचर्मभिः । Ibid., Udyoga, 152.6.
128. Ibid., Droṇa, 131.26.
129. Ibid., Udyoga, 152.3-12.
130. Ibid., Droṇa, 156.57-61 (BE).
131. *Rām*, Yuddha, 106.1-8.
132. *Mbh*, Droṇa, 8.8; also see Karṇa, 26.56, 26.74, 56.11; Udyoga, 152.6; Sabhā, 47.29.
133. Ibid., Droṇa, 8.8.
134. Hopkins, op. cit., p. 211.
135. द्वावङ्कुशधरौ तेषु द्वावुत्तमधनुर्धरौ ।
द्वौ वरासिधरौ राजन्नेकः शक्तिपताकधृक् ।। *Mbh*, Udyoga, 152.14.
136. सर्वमायुधकेतुभिः । Ibid., Droṇa, 48.28.
नागानां मभिरूपाणां वर्मिणां रौद्रकर्मिणाम् । Ibid., 63.18.
137. गजाः कङ्कटसंन्नाहा लोहवर्मोत्तरच्छदाः । Ibid., 149.82.
138. कांस्यायसतनुत्राणान् । Ibid., 31.17.
तस्यायसं वर्मवरं वररत्नविभूषितम् । Ibid., Karṇa, 8.23, also 12.60.
139. गजानां पार्श्वचर्माणि गोवृषाजगराणि च ।
शल्यकङ्कटलोहानि तनुत्राणि मतानि च ।। Ibid., Śānti, 101.6.
140. तद्वर्म व्यधमत् । Ibid., Droṇa, 28.8.
141. वर्माणि अशातयत् । Ibid., Droṇa, 36.34-35 (BE).
142. द्विपाः संभिन्नमवर्माणो । Ibid., Karṇa, 14.12; also 59.25.
143. Hopkins, op. cit., p. 212; also see *Mbh*, Droṇa, 91.47.
144. Ibid., Karṇa, 17.107.
145. Hopkins, op. cit., p. 212.
146. तोत्रैरिव महानागं कशाभिरिव वाजिनम् । *Mbh*, Droṇa, 109.6.
तोत्राङ्कुशनिपाताश्च आयुधानां च निस्वनाः । Ibid., Bhīṣma, 43.5.
147. तोत्राङ्कुशैः प्रेषयामास तूर्णं । Ibid., Śalya, 19.15.
148. पुनर्द्विपान् द्विपारोहान् वैजयन्त्यङ्कुशध्वजान् ।
तूणान् वर्माण्यथो कक्ष्या ग्रैवेयानथ कम्बलान् ।।

घण्टाः शुण्डान्विषाणाग्रान् क्षुरपालान्पदानुगान् ।
शरैर्निशितधाराग्रैः शात्रवाणामशातयत् ।। Ibid., Droṇa, 35.34-35, also, 73.25-27; Karṇa, 94.19-20; Bhīṣma, 50.48-51.

149. Hopkins, op. cit., pp. 206-7.
150. रुक्मपत्रैरुरच्छदैः । *Mbh*, Droṇa, 22.29.
अश्वाना रत्नचित्रानुरच्छदान् । Ibid., 19.46 (BE).
151. चामरापीडकवचाः । Ibid., 18.31.
निकृत्तवर्मकवचान् । Ibid., 35.39.
152. वैयाध्रैर्हेमचन्द्रकैः । Ibid., 79.5.
153. विचित्रान्मणिचित्रांश्च जातरूपपरिष्कृतान् । Ibid., Karṇa, 14.48; हेमचन्द्रकैः। Ibid., Droṇa, 79.5; स्वर्णजालपरिच्छदाः । Ibid., 22.41.
154. Ibid., Karṇa, 17.107.
155. Ibid., Bhīṣma, 92.72.
156. हीना आस्तरणैश्चैव खलीनैश्च विवर्जिताः ।
चामरैश्च कुथाभिश्च तुणीरैः पतितैरपि ।। Ibid., Karṇa, 17.107.
157. तोत्रैरिव महानागं कशाभिरिव वाजिनम् । Ibid., Droṇa, 109.6; Karṇa, 16.21.
158. वद्धाः सादिभुजाग्रेषु सुवर्णविकृताः कशाः । Ibid., Karṇa, 14.47.
159. Ibid., Droṇa 35.36-39, 18.26-27; Karṇa, 17.106-07.

CHAPTER 6

Maurya-Śuṅga Age

PRE-MAURYAN COSTUME

Herodotus, the Greek historian, has made a specific reference to military costume of India in the fifth century BC. He has recorded that the Indian military contingent which had joined the army of Persian king Xerxes (486-465 BC) during his invasion of Greece was clad in cotton garments and carried bows and arrows of cane, the latter tipped with iron. The Indian cavalry was armed with the same equipment as infantry, but they had also brought along riding horses and chariots, the latter being drawn by horses and wild asses.[1]

GREEK EVIDENCE

A clearer picture of Indian military costume in the fourth century BC emerges from the writings of Greek historians. Relevant extracts from their writings are quoted below:

1. Among Oxydrakai (Kṣudraka people) 'kings on going forth to war and on other occasions marched in Bacchic fashion, with drums beating, while they were dressed in gay coloured robes, which is also a custom among other Indians'.[2]
2. The Sibae (Śivi) people, who lived around the confluence of Chenab and Jhelum and whom the Macedonians considered as the followers of Herakles, 'preserved badges of their descent, for they wore skins

like Herakles, and carried clubs, and branded the mark of a cudgel on their oxen and mules'.[3]

3. The people of the hill state of Nysa, inhabiting the lower spurs and valley of the Koh-i-Mor, followed the practice of 'marching to battle with drums and cymbals, and of wearing a spotted dress such as was worn by the Bacchanals of Dionysos'.[4]
4. 'The Indians were in old times nomadic like those Scythians who did not till the soil... but were so barbarous that they wore the skins of such wild animals as they could kill.'[5]
5. 'The dress worn by the Indians is made of cotton.... But this cotton is either of a brighter white colour than any cotton found elsewhere, or the darkness of Indian complexion makes their apparel look so much the whiter. They wear an under-garment of cotton which reaches below the knee halfway down to the ankles, and also an upper garment which they throw partly over their shoulders, and partly twist in folds round their head.'[6]
6. 'They cover their person down to the feet with fine muslin, are shod with sandals, and coil round their heads cloths of linen (cotton). They hang precious stones as pendants from their ears and persons of high social rank, or of great wealth, deck their wrist and upper arm with bracelets of gold. They frequently comb, but seldom cut, the hair of their head. The beard of the chin they never cut at all, but they shave off the hair from the rest of the face, so that it looks polished.'[7]
7. 'They (Indians) wear shoes made of white leather, and these are elaborately trimmed while the soles are variegated, and made of great thickness to make the wearer seem much taller.'[8] The *Aṣṭādhyāyī* also refers to a kind of boot which covered the whole foot and was tied at the ankles.[9]

The references to Indian costume in classical accounts suggest that people generally wore a upper garment (*uttarīya*), a lower garment (*adhovāsa*), a turban (*uṣṇīṣa*) and shoes. The soldiers may also have dressed in a like manner. Some tribals in north-west India may also have used skin garment.

WEAPONS AND EQUIPMENT

Arrian has described the weapons of Indian soldier in detail:

I proceed now to describe the mode in which the Indians equip themselves for war premising that it is not to be regarded as the only one in vogue. The foot-soldiers carry a bow made of equal length with the man who bears it. This they rest upon the ground, and pressing against it with their left foot thus discharge the arrow, having drawn the string far backwards: for the shaft they use is little short of being three yards long, and there is nothing which can resist an Indian archer's shot—neither shield nor breastplate, nor any stronger defence if such there be. In their left hand they carry bucklers made of undressed ox-hide, which are not so broad as those who carry them, but are about as long. Some are equipped with javelins instead of bows, but all wear a sword, which is broad in the blade, but not longer than three cubits; and this when they engage in close fight (which they do with reluctance), they wield with both hands to fetch down a lustier blow. The horsemen are equipped with two lances like the lances called *saunia*, and with a shorter buckler than that carried by foot-soldiers.[10]

Arrian has also made some observations on the equipment of the horse:

But they do not put saddles on their horses, nor do they curb them with bits like the bits in use among the Greeks or the Kelts, but they fit on round the extremity of the horse's mouth a circular piece of stitched raw ox-hide studded with pricks of iron or brass pointing inwards, but not very sharp: if a man is rich he uses pricks made of ivory. Within the horses mouth is put an iron prong like a skewer, to which the reins are attached. When the rider, then, pulls the reins, the prong controls the horse, and the pricks which are attached to this prong goad the mouth so that it cannot but obey the reins.[11]

The war elephant was equipped with a tower, which carried four men—three who shot arrows, and the driver. The driver carried a goad to guide the animal.[12]

A chariot was drawn by four horses and carried two men besides the charioteer.[13]

Thus it appears that in fourth century BC a foot-soldier carried a bow, a javelin and a sword for weapon. The cavalry soldier carried a sword and two lances. All carried a shield, which in the case of cavalrymen was shorter.

The rise of the Maurya dynasty ushered in far-reaching changes in the military set-up of India. Mauryans maintained a large army, comprising 600,000 infantry, 30,000 cavalry, 9,000 elephants and 8,000 chariots. Though these numbers appear to be highly exaggerated it can be said with certainty that the Mauryans maintained the largest standing army in the world at that time. Significantly, this army was maintained at the state expense and the soldiers were paid salaries in cash. Close contact with the Greeks may also have influenced the Mauryan army set up, particularly in respect of dress and equipment.

STATE'S RESPONSIBILITY

The state provided for the costume and accoutrements of the soldiers. Describing the class composition of Indian society Megasthenese observes:

The fifth class (of the Indians) consists of fighting men, who, when not engaged in active service pass their time in idleness and drinking. They are maintained at the king's expense and hence they are always ready, when occasion calls, to take the field, for they carry nothing of their own with them but their own bodies.[14]

This clearly suggests that 'the Mauryan kings maintained a regular standing army, as they seems to have provided their soldiers with arms and uniform, as well as pay'.[15] The *Arthaśāstra* says that the state maintained a department for this purpose.[16]

ĀYUDHĀGĀRĀDHYAKṢA (SUPERINTENDENT OF ARMOURY)

Āyudhāgārādhyakṣa was responsible for the manufacture and maintenance of weapons and armour. The *Arthaśāstra* says:

[He] should cause to be made machines for use in battle, for the defence of forts and for assault on the enemies' cities, also weapons, armours, and accoutrements by artisans and artists expert in those lines, producing goods with an agreement as to the amount of work, time allowed and wages, and should store them in places suitable for each. He should frequently change their places and expose them to sun and wind. He should store in a different way that is being damaged by heat, moisture or insects. And he should know them by their class, appearance, characteristics, quantity, source, price, and place of storing.[17]

The soldiers were issued arms from the armoury when required. Strabo says that there are royal stables for the horses and elephants and also a royal magazine for the arms, because the soldier has to return his arms to the magazine and his horse and his elephant to the stables.[18] It seems that all arms kept in the royal armoury were stamped with the king's insignia.[19] The scabbard of the sword borne by a soldier in Bhārhut art bears a *tri-ratna* symbol.[20] This symbol also figures on the royal standards depicted in Bhārhut, Sāñcī and Amarāvatī art.

SŪTRĀDHYAKṢA (SUPERINTENDENT OF YARNS)

Another officer called Superintendent of Yarns, was responsible for the production of military costume and equipment.[21] He was expected to get yarn spun out of wool, bark-fibres, cotton, silk, hemp and flax[22] and 'cause trade to be carried out in yarn, armour (*varma*), cloth and rope'.[23] This large scale production of yarns, etc., under state control must have been intended to serve a military purpose. In this connection it is notable that the production of *varma*, a kind of armour, was the responsibility of *sūtrādhyakṣa. Kaṅkaṭa*, again a type of armour was made of yarn. It was in great demand and factories were opened for its production.[24]

Sūtrādhyakṣa was expected to supervise the production of armour and ropes personally[25] and 'to cause ropes to be made of yarn and fibres, (and) thongs of canes and bamboos, as trappings for war and bindings for vehicles and draught animals'.[26] The superintendent of horse was to ensure that 'qualified teachers shall give instructions as to the manufacture of proper ropes with which to tether the horses'.[27]

ARMOUR (*KAVACA*)

In connection with Indian soldiers the armour is rarely spoken of by the Greek historians. But King Poros has been described as dressed in an armour and he was 'wounded in the right shoulder, where only he was unprotected by armour in the battle. All the rest of his person was rendered shot-proof by his coat of mail, which was remarkable for its strength and the closeness with which it fitted his person.'[28]

The *Arthaśāstra* refers to various kinds of armour made of iron (*loha*), fabrics (*paṭṭa*), and skins (*carma*) of various animals. Armour included helmet (*śirastrāṇa*), neck-guard (*kaṇṭhatrāṇa*), cuirass (*kūrpāsa*), robe (*kañcuka*), coat of mail (*varavāṇa*), thigh-guard (*nāgodarika*), etc.[29] But the armoured soldier is rarely depicted in early Indian art. In Sāñcī sculptures, only one representation of breast-plate is met in a panel depicting the march of an army.[30] It is decorated with three bands, a vertical one in the centre and two oblique, crossing each other in the middle. This near total absence of armour in war scenes at Sāñcī is indeed difficult to explain.

SHIELD (*CARMAN*)

Soldiers carried various types of shields made of leather, wood, or cane on their person. According to Arrian the Indian shields, made of undressed ox-hide, were not sufficiently broad to cover the bearer but were long enough to match his height.[31] These could be equated with the *kavāṭa* shield of the *Arthaśāstra*, which resembled a door-leaf.[32]

In the Sāñcī sculptures four types of shields are represented. The first type which is oblong and rounded at the top, appears in different sizes. The second type is triangular in shape and rounded at the top. The third type is round and basket shaped and the fourth is rectangular with three cuts at the upper end.[33]

The large-sized oblong shields, represented in the war scenes, provided complete protection to the bearer. These are three and a half feet in length and one and a half feet in breadth.[34] The outer face of the shields is adorned with cross-bands and other motifs. It seems that the length of Indian shield had now shortened by about a feet compared to the one used in the fourth century BC. The shield carried by horsemen was about two feet in length. Occasionally,

Plate 4: Maurya soldier

it was shaped like a bell with a wide mouth, and rounded at the bottom.[35]

The representations in Sāñcī panels suggest that shield was basically an infantry weapon used by swordsmen and lancers. The material used in making shields is not known but going by the evidence of the *Arthaśāstra* these could have been made of wood, cane or hide.[36]

SWORD (*ASI*)

In fourth century BC a heavy sword was a popular weapon. According to Arrian 'all (soldiers) bear a sword, which is broad in the blade; but not longer than three cubits; and this, when they engage in close fight (which they do with reluctance) they wield with both hands, to fetch down a lustier blow'.[37] But in the *Arthaśāstra* three sword types, viz., *nistriṁśa* (curved tip), *maṇḍalāgra* (straight with round tip) and *asiyaṣṭi* (thin and long) are mentioned.[38] The sword-hilts were made of rhino and buffalo horn, elephant tusk, wood or bamboo-root.[39]

The heavy sword depicted in a Bhārhut sculpture seems to represent the type referred to by Greek historians. Cunningham has described it in detail.

The soldier carries in his right a monstrously broad straight sword, sheathed in a scabbard, which is suspended from the left shoulder by a long flat belt. The extreme breadth of the sword may be judged by comparing it with the thickness of the man's arm, which it exceeds, while its length may be about 2½ feet, or perhaps somewhat more. The belt of the sword is straight and without a guard. The face of the scabbard is ornamented with the famous Buddhist Omega symbol of *tri-ratna*, or the triple jem. The sword belt, after being passed through a ring attached to the side of the scabbard, appears to be twice crossed over the scabbard downwards, and then fastened to a ring at the tip, below which the broad ends hang down like the end of a scarf.[40] (Figure 3)

Figure 3: Warrior, Bhārhut

But the swords represented in Sāñcī reliefs are generally short and broad (Figure 4).[41]

BOW (*DHANUṢ*)

In the fourth century BC Indian foot-soldiers carried a bow, long enough to match the height of the bearer.

> This they rest upon the ground, and pressing against it with their left foot thus discharge the arrow, having drawn the string far backwards: for the shaft they use is little short of being three yards long, and there is nothing which can resist an Indian archer's shot—neither shield, nor breastplate nor any stronger defence if such there be.[42]

However, Curtius has no praise for the Indian arrow shot. 'The arrows, which are two cubits long, are discharged with more effort than effect, for though the force of these missiles depends on their lightness they are loaded with an obnoxious weight.'[43]

The *Arthaśāstra* refers to four bow types, viz., *kārmuka, dhanu*, *drūṇa* and *kodaṇḍa* made of wood or horn.[44] The bow-string was made of some grass or sinews. The arrows were made of reed or iron. If made of reed these were provided with iron or bone tips.[45] The arrow types included *veṇu, śara, śalākā, daṇḍāsana* and *narāca.*[46]

The long bow referred to by Arrian is also represented in the art of Sāñcī.[47] But gradually a shorter bow, about four feet in length, seems to have come into greater vogue.[48] Most of the bows appear to be straight pieces of bamboo, but a few have the double curve, with a straight hand-piece in the middle, similar to modern ornamental bows of buffalo's horn (Figure 5).[49]

The archers carried a quiver.

> [At Sāñcī] the mode of fastening quiver to the back is very peculiar and picturesque. The quiver is fastened to the right shoulder, and the fastenings, which are apparently leather straps,

Figure 4: Soldiers in action, Sāñcī

are passed over both shoulders, crossed in front, and carried to the back, where they were probably passed through a ring in the end of the quiver, and then carried to the front and again crossed, the ends being secured by loops to the upper straps.[50] (Figure 5)

SCULPTURAL EVIDENCE

The contemporary sculptures at Bhārhut, Sāñcī and Amarāvatī represent the military costume of the age. In this connection the reliefs depicting royal processions and war scenes at Sāñcī[51] and Amarāvatī[52] yield some valuable information.

HEADDRESS (*ŚIROVASTRA*)

Soldiers are generally shown wearing a turban in Bhārhut and Sāñcī sculptures. However, some distinction in the size and shape of the turban worn by high ranking commanders and common soldiers is discernible. The former appear in fluffy and elaborately adorned turbans while the latter appear in simple turbans.[53] Occasionally, soldiers are shown bare-headed.

GARMENTS (*VASTRA*)

In fourth century BC the Indian soldier used an *uttarīya* for upper garment and a *dhotī* for lower garment. These remained in vogue during the Maurya-Śuṅga period as well. In the art of Sāñcī the soldiers generally appear without an *uttarīya* though *dhotī* continued to be in use.[54] In Sāñcī, a set of soldiers is represented in kilt and tunic, undoubtedly a dress style introduced by foreigners.[55] Archers dona cross-belt on the chest.[56]

WAIST-BAND (*KAṬIBANDHA*)

Almost all soldiers depicted in Sāñcī art appear in a waist-band. Though a common dress item of the period it was

Figure 5: Archers, Sāñcī

worn intertwined like a thick rope around the waist in the case of soldiers. It seems that the swordsmen donned a bigger waist-band coiled around the waist six or seven times.[57] In the case of horsemen it was shorter with four or five coils.[58] Some soldiers also appear in waist-bands worn in one or two coils.[59] Perhaps, a lavish waist-band denoted the higher status of the person (Figure 5).

Shoes (*Upānaha*)

The type of the boots referred to by Arrian may have continued in use during the Maurya-Śuṅga period. But the shoe types represented in the art of Bhārhut and Sāñcī appear to be of foreign make.[60]

Coiffeur (*Keśa vinyāsa*)

In fourth century BC, Indians donned long hair. If Arrian is right in quoting Megasthenese, 'they (Indians) frequently comb, but seldom cut, hair of their head. The beard of the chin they never cut at all but they shave off the hair from the rest of the face, so that it looks polished.'[61] He adds that Indians dye their beards in one hue or another, according to taste. 'Some dye their white beards to make them look as white as possible, but others dye them blue; while some again prefer a red tint, some a purple and others a rank green.'[62] Surprisingly, soldiers are seldom seen with beards in the Sāñcī art suggesting that the fashion was no more in vogue. The fashion of keeping long hair, however, continued.

VEHICLES OF WAR

Chariot (*Ratha*)

Chariot, elephant and horse were the main vehicles of war during the Maurya-Śuṅga period. In the fourth century BC the Indian war-chariot generally carried three persons, two warriors and one charioteer.[63] Occasionally, the chariot carried as many as six men:

> Its (Poros's army) main strength lay in the chariot, each of which was drawn by four horses and carried six men of whom two were shield-bearers, two archers posted on each side of the chariot, and the other two, charioteers, as well as men-at-arms, for when the fighting was at close-quarters they dropped the reins and hurled dart after dart against the enemy.[64]

In the battle of Jhelum, Poros was accompanied by three hundred chariots.[65]

A Sāñcī panel depicts a chariot occupied by three persons.[66] But generally the Sāñcī chariot is represented as carrying two persons, the warrior and the charioteer only (Figure 6).[67] The war chariot was made six feet high and seven and a half feet long.[68]

It may be recalled here that Pāṇini has also referred to the use of chariot in war.[69] After fabrication, it was

Figure 6: Chariot, Sāñcī

upholstered with cloth (*vastra*), blanket (*kaṁbala*), or leather (*carma*). A chariot mounted with a special woollen stuff named *pāṇḍukaṁbala* (yellow blanket) was called *pāṇḍu-kaṁbalī*. Similarly, chariots covered with leopard and tiger skins were called *dvaupa* and *vaiyāghra* respectively.[70] The Jātakas also refer to such chariots.[71] Subsequently, the names *śatāṅga, syandana* and *ratha* came to be applied to war chariot.[72] The protective screen of the chariot was called *varūtha*.[73]

ELEPHANT (*HASTIN*)

The elephant was another important vehicle of war. In the battle of Jhelum, Poros deployed two hundred elephants against the army of Alexander.[74] He himself fought mounted on an elephant.[75] The army of Candragupta Maurya included nine thousand elephants. According to Megasthenese a war elephant carried three archers and a driver,[76] but in Sāñcī reliefs elephants are shown carrying only three persons.[77]

The equipment of an elephant included a howdah, girth, ornaments, decorated coverings, bells and ropes. Rings were put around the ankles.[78] The goad held by the driver (*mahāmātra*) was a rod with a metallic hook.[79]

Girth (*kakṣya*) was a thick rope fastened around the body of the elephant and tightly knotted on the sides.[80] Occasionally, a lighter rope was attached to it to help the rider. It was either fastened around the body or held in hand by the rider (Figure 7).[81] Some other methods of tying the girth were also practised.[82]

The elephant was provided with two coverings, one for the neck and the other for the back. The first was an ornamental piece of cloth thrown in folds over the neck.[83] The second was a well designed large covering with ends

Figure 7: Caparisoned elephants, Sāñcī

adorned with tassels.[84] The elephant was also provided with a skull-band, an ornamental piece made either of metal or heavy drapery, which was tied to the forehead.[85]

The *Arthaśāstra* provides some interesting information on the paraphernalia of the elephant. The tying-post, neck-chain, girth, stirrup rope, post-chain, upper chain, etc., constituted the tying equipment. The goad, bamboo, machine, etc., were implements. The *vaijayanta* (garland), covering, carpet, etc., were ornaments. The armour, lance, knife quiver, machines, etc., were weapons and accoutrements of war.[86] The superintendent of elephants ensured proper arrangement of straps, implements, and accoutrements for war elephants[87] as per the instructions of the trainer.[88]

Horse (*Aśva*)

The horse had become an important vehicle of war by the fourth century BC. The army of Poros included four thousand horses.[89] In Sāñcī reliefs horses are represented in full equipment, including rein (*yoktra, valga*), bridle (*khalīna*), girth (*kakṣya*), saddle (*paristoma*), whip (*kaṣā*), stirrup, etc. (Figures 8, 9).[90] The trainers were to ensure proper use of straps (*bandhana*) and equipment (*upa-karaṇa*) of the horses.[91]

The rein was attached to the lower band of the head-stall with the help of a strap, perhaps made of leather. According to Cunningham 'it is quite possible that the bridle was introduced between the time of Alexander and Aśoka'.[92] But the bridle was actually known to Indians even before the invasion of Alexander.[93] Bridles of various designs are represented in the art of Bhārhut[94] and Sāñcī.[95] The head-stall to which the bridle was attached was made in three horizontal bands though in some cases two bands are also met. It is said that 'where bits are used, the horses have but two bands in their head-stall. But when the spike (behind the jaw) is intended, the head-stall has three bands, one passing over the nostrils, another beneath and a third above the eyes.'[96]

Bit (*Khalina*)

Though the curb-bit was not known to Indians in fourth century BC it was known to them in first century BC.[97] Perhaps, it came into vogue in Maurya-Śuṅga period as a result of Greek influence. The hypothesis that *kharkhalina* (curb-bit), a Sanskrit word for bit, was borrowed from Greek language[98] also strengthens this supposition.

But there is also evidence to suggest that bits were known in India much before the invasion of Alexandar. In this connection the observations made by Bridget and Raymond Allchin regarding the objects discovered from the southern peninsular megalith sites are notable.

> Another special group of objects includes horse furniture. In several of the graves around Nagpur, Junapani, Khapa Mahurjhari

Figure 8: Caparisoned horses, Sāñcī

Figure 9: Mounted standard-bearer, Bhārhut

and Naikund, iron snaffle bits have been found, some with iron cheek pieces: one bit was found in the mouth of a buried horse [fig. 12.20 (b)]. There were also simple bar-bits of iron with looped end.[99]

Many more types have been discovered from other places, including Gandhāra.[100]

GIRTH (*KAKṢYA*)

The girth was integral to horse's equipment. It passed vertically or horizontally around the body of the horse and served as a link between the carriage and the horse. When drawing a chariot the tail of the horse was also tied to the girth so that it did not get into the rotating wheel.[101] Subsequently, a vertical belt which passed underneath the belly of the horse and firmed up the saddle also became a part of the girth.[102] Senior commanders of the army ornamented the girth of their horse with auspicious symbols like *śrīvatsa.*[103]

The Greek sources are silent about the use of saddle by Indians in the fourth century BC. Bhārhut sculptures also do not portray a saddle.[104] A rare representation of saddle in Sāñcī[105] seems to suggest some foreign influence. However, the Indian horsemen might have put some kind of covering on the horseback for comfortable riding.

The stirrup, the earliest specimen of which is met at Sāñcī, was unknown during the Maurya-Śuṅga period and was perhaps introduced in India by the mounted bowmen of the steppes.[106] These early stirrups were indeed made of rope or leather strap as the metal stirrups came much later. The horse was adorned in accordance with the status of the owner. *Cāmara*, necklace and bangles were included in its adornments.

A general survey of military costume and accoutrements in the Maurya-Śuṅga period suggests no break with the past as *śiroveṣṭana*, *vastra* or *vasana* (upper garment), and *ambara* (lower garment) continued to be in use. But unlike the Epic times the use of armour does not appear to be common in the Maurya-Śuṅga age. The use of kilt and tunic by the soldiers in the art of Sāñcī was indeed a Greek impact.

NOTES

1. E.J. Rapson, *Cambridge History of India*, vol. 1, pp. 305-6.
2. J.W. M'Crindle, *Ancient India as described by Megasthenese and Arrian*, p. 110.
3. Ibid., pp. 111, 196.
4. Ibid., p. 195.
5. Ibid., p. 199.
6. Ibid., p. 219.
7. J.W. M'Crindle, *The Invasion of India by Alexander the Great*, p. 188.
8. Ibid.; also *Ancient India*, p. 220.
9. *Aṣṭādhyāyī*, 5.2.6; In *Vinaya* texts sandals, slippers, shoes and boots of various colours are referred to. B.C. Law, *Indological Studies*, vol. 1, p. 113.
10. M'Crindle, *Ancient India*, pp. 220-1.
11. Ibid., p. 221; also p. 89.
12. Ibid., pp. 89-90.
13. Ibid., p. 90.
14. Ibid., p. 85.
15. A. Cunningham, *The Stūpa of Bhārhut*, p. 33.
16. *Arthaśāstra*, 2.18.
17. Ibid., 2.18.1-4.
18. M'Crindle, *Ancient India*, p. 88.
19. *Arthaśāstra*, 5.3.37; According to B.C. Law 'there is no trace of defensive armour' in pre-Nanda period, *Indological Studies*, vol. 1, p. 69.
20. Cunningham, *The Stūpa of Bhārhut*, pp. 32-3.
21. सूत्राध्यक्षः सूत्रवर्मवस्त्ररज्जुव्यवहारं तज्जातपुरुषैः कारयेत्। *Arthaśāstra*, 2.23.1.
22. ऊर्णावल्ककार्पासतूलशणक्षौमाणि। Ibid., 2.23.2.

23. Ibid., 2.23.1.
24. कङ्कटकर्मान्तांश्च तज्जातकारुशिल्पिभि: कारयेत्। Ibid., 2.23.10. According to Kangle this armour may have been made of wool or other cloth filled with cotton or other stuffing, p. 147 fn.
25. रज्जुवर्तकैर्वर्मकारैश्च स्वयं संसृज्येत। Ibid., 2.23.17.
26. Ibid., 2.23.19.
27. तेषां वन्धनोपकरणं योग्याचार्य: प्रतिदिशेयु: । Ibid., 2.30.42.
28. M'Crindle, *The Invasion of India*, p. 108.
29. लोहजालिकापट्टकवचसूत्रकङ्कटशिंशुमारक खड्गिधेनुकहस्तिगोचर्मखुरशृङ्ग संघातं वर्माणि। शिरस्त्राणकण्ठत्राणकूर्पासकञ्चुकवारवाणपट्टनागोदरिका:। *Arthaśāstra*, 2.18.16-17 and fn.
30. G.N. Pant, *Indian Arms and Armour*, p. 21, pl. 15.
31. M'Crindle, *Ancient India*, p. 221.
32. *Arthaśāstra*, 2.18.17; The other types mentioned in the *Arthaśāstra* include *carma*, *hastikarṇa*, *dhamanikā*, *kīṭika*, *apratihata* and *balāhakanta*. Ibid., 2.18.17.
33. A. Cunningham, *The Bhilsā Topes*, pl. 33; J. Marshall and A. Foucher, *The Monuments of Sāñcī*, pl. 15.3.
34. Cunningham, *The Bhilsa Topes*, p. 139.
35. Ibid.
36. *Arthaśāstra*, 2.18.17.
37. M'Crindle, *Ancient India*, p. 221.
38. *Arthaśāstra*, 2.18.12.
39. Ibid., 2.18.13
40. Cunningham, *The Stūpa of Bhārhut*, pp. 32-3.
41. Cunninghan, *The Bhilsā Topes*, p. 138, pl. 32.2.
42. M'Crindle, *Ancient India*, pp. 220-1.
43. M'Crindle, *The Invasion of India*, p. 188.
44. *Arthaśāstra*, 2.18.8.
45. Ibid., 2.18.11.
46. Ibid., 2.18.10.
47. Marshall and Foucher, *The Monuments of Sāñchī*, pl. 65 (top left).
48. Ibid., pl., 15.3; Cunningham, *The Bhilsā Topes*, p. 139.
49. Cunningham, *The Bhilsā Topes*, p. 139.
50. Ibid., p. 138; Marshall and Foucher, op. cit., p. 153.
51. Marshall and Foucher, op. cit., pl. 11 (middle), pl. 40 (middle and lower); also pl. 15.3.
52. C. Sivaramamurti, *Amarāvatī*, pl. 45, fig. 1.
53. Marshall and Foucher, op. cit., pl. 11, 39, 40.

54. Ibid., pl. 15.3 (right).
55. Ibid., pl. 15.3 (left).
56. Ibid., pl. 65a.
57. Ibid., pl. 15.3 (centre).
58. Ibid.
59. Ibid.
60. Ibid., pl. 36c; Cunningham, *The Stūpa of Bhārhut*, pl. 32.4.
61. M'Crindle, *The Invasion of India*, p. 188, fn. 2.
62. M'Crindle, *Ancient India*, p. 220; also J. Fergusson, *Tree and Serpent Worship*, p. 93.
63. M'Crindle, *Ancient India*, p. 89.
64. M'Crindle, *The Invasion of India*, p. 207.
65. Ibid., pp. 101-2.
66. Marshall and Foucher, op. cit., pl. 11 (centre).
67. Ibid., pl. 15.3.
68. *Arthaśāstra*, 2.33.4-5.
69. V.S. Agrawala, *India as Known to Pāṇini*, p. 148.
70. Ibid., pp. 149-50; *Amarakośa* (2.8.53-54) adds that chariots covered with वस्त्र and दुकूल were called वास्त्र and दौकूल respectively.
71. E.B. Cowell, *The Jātaka*, vol. 6, pp. 48-50.
72. *Amarakośa*, 2.8.51.
73. Ibid., 2.8.57.
74. M'Crindle, *The Invasion of India*, pp. 102-3.
75. Ibid., p. 108.
76. Ibid., p. 89.
77. Marshall and Foucher, op. cit., pl. 11.
78. B.M. Barua, *Bhārhut*, Figs. 75, 77, 148, etc.
79. F.C. Maisey, *Sāñchī and Its Remains*, pl. 20.
80. Marshall and Foucher, op. cit., pls. 44, 57.
81. Ibid., pl. 57 (top).
82. Krishnadas Rai, *Journal of UP Historical Society*, vol. 18, pl. 1.
83. Marshall and Foucher, op. cit., pls. 16, 23, etc.
84. Ibid., pls. 23,57.
85. Barua, op. cit., Figs. 62, 79, 148.
86. *Arthaśāstra*, 2.32.11-15; also Cowell, op. cit., vol. 6, p. 253.
87. Ibid., 2.31.1.
88. Ibid., 2.32.11.
89. M'Crindle, *The Invasion of India*, p. 102.
90. Marshall and Foucher, op. cit., pls. 22 (centre), 58.3, etc.
91. *Arthaśāstra*, 2.30.42.

92. Cunningham, *The Stūpa of Bhārhut*, p. 42.
93. M'Crindle, *Ancient India*, p. 221.
94. Ibid., pls. 12, 20.
95. Marshall, and Foucher, op. cit., pls. 22, 31, 58.
96. P.C. Chakravarti, *The Art of War in Ancient India*, p. 38; also Cunningham, *The Stūpa of Bhārhut*, p. 43.
97. Marshall and Foucher, op. cit., pl. 23; Fergusson, however, doubts the very presence of bit in the art of Sāñchī. *Tree and Serpent Worship*, p. 134.
98. V.S. Agrawala, *Harṣacarita: Eka Sāṁskṛtika Adhyayana*, pp. 20-1.
99. Bridget and Raymond Allchin, *The Rise of Civilization in India and Pakistan*, p. 336.
100. Ibid., pp. 311-12, 336.
101. Marshall and Foucher, op. cit., pl. 23a.
102. Ibid., pls. 28 (middle), 31.
103. Ibid., pl. 22.
104. Cunningham, *The Stūpa of Bhārhut*, p. 42, pls. 12, 20.
105. Marshall and Foucher, op. cit., pl. 97.
106. For details see next Chapter.

CHAPTER 7

Śaka-Kuṣāṇa Age

The decline of the Maurya empire synchronized with large scale invasions leading to foreign occupation of northern India and parts of Deccan. Among the foreigners the Greeks, the Śakas and the Kuṣāṇas exercised political authority over large parts of the country around the beginning of the Christian era. The weight of the Greek arms was felt as far east as Sāketa, though their political influence remained confined to western parts of India. During Kaniṣka's reign Kuṣāṇa power stretched from Bihar in the east to Khorasan in the west and from Khotan in the north to Ujjayinī in the south. The Śakas, who had entered India before the Kuṣāṇas and had carved out some independent principalities and subsequently became their vassals, also exercised considerable political authority in India.

FOREIGN IMPACT

Foreign invaders introduced a new set of military costume and accoutrements in India.

the coin portraits of (the Śaka rulers) Maues and Azes 1 (text figure 15; coins 269,270) show the princes heavily armoured somewhat in the manner of the Persian cataphracti. . . . The Persian riders wore helmets, and both they and their horses were protected with chain-mail or with body-plates of metal or leather. A long spear and a long sword were the basic offensive weapons. According to historical records this armament was used by the aristocrats among the Sarmatians of south Russia and the Parthians of Iran, whereas their retainers were armed with bows and arrows and comprised the light cavalry. This was a formidable tactical system, which the Sassanians also used and which the Romans both feared and emulated. The Indo-Śaka princes are shown in much the same guise on their coins, except that their horses appear not to have had the same degree of protection.[1]

The Śaka armies comprised mounted archers, mobile light cavalry, and heavily armoured spear bearers. This combination was also used effectively by Parthians and Sarmatians. The heavy cavalry was usually drawn from the higher ranks of aristocracy.[2]

In the Gandhāra art many Śaka-Kuṣāṇa soldiers appear dressed in their native costume. To illustrate, in a Gandhāra sculpture a warrior wears a double skirted cuirass over a tunic reaching the knees. This piece of protection consists of imbricated mail below, and above, coming up to the chest a sort of waist coat, probably of leather and tied in front. On his feet are high boots; in his left hand he holds a figure-8 shield.[3]

Another sculpture (Figure 10) represents some warriors armed with spears and swords, favourite weapons of the Kuṣāṇas. Two warriors are shown in scale armour. The warrior on the right wears a helmet. Rippling folds appear on the undergarment of the warrior on the left. The latter is depicted without shoes whereas the former is shown in shoes.[4]

A seal portraying an equestrian depicts a Kuṣāṇa in tunic and pantaloons seated on doll-like horse. He wears a low cap with fillets streaming behind, and holds a peculiar device in the left hand, which could be either a pointed goad or a kind of insignia. The rider has stirrup-like foot support attached to the saddle.[5]

The numismatic evidence also adds to our understanding of the Kuṣāṇa costume. The portrayal of Kaniṣka on a coin has been described as follows:

Figure 10: Armed warriors, Gandhāra

King wearing low rounded cap of uncertain design, standing to left sacrificing over low rounded altar. In left hand is spear. Has long untidy beard. Dressed in long tunic, shalwars and some kind of anklet, and mantle held by double clasp at the chest. Armed also with sword whose pommel is shaped like an animal neck and head. Wears belt with a double-unit buckle. Flames emanate from right shoulder.[6]

The statue of Kaniṣka at Mathurā also yields valuable information on Kuṣāṇa costume (Figure 11). In this connection the portrayal of two bearded sentries wearing Roman helmet and a long quilted tunic and pantaloons on stone pillars at Vijayapurī is significant. Longhurst believes that these sculptures represent the Scythian royal body-guards, of whom a colony might have existed at Vijayapurī in the second or third century AD.[7]

In this context it is notable that the Śaka-Kuṣāṇa coat, as represented on the coins of Wema Kadphises,[8] was made of coarse and heavy woollen cloth. Kaniṣka has also been represented in almost similar coat in an sculpture at Mathurā.[9] The coat was designed in full sleeves to fit in well at the waist and fall down to the calfs like an inverted 'V' letter.

A general survey of the sculptures and coins belonging to the Śaka-Kuṣāṇa period reveals that the costume of the immigrants was undisputedly non-Indian. Still, despite its unsuitability for Indian climatic conditions it survived and even flourished with some modifications in fabric and design.

BHĀRHUT SOLDIER

The costume and accoutrements of Indian soldier was greatly influenced by the Greek and Śaka-Kuṣāṇa invaders. In the battle of Jhelum the Indian soldier had appeared in a loose upper garment.[10] But a coat like garment appeared

Figure 11: Kaniṣka in battle-dress

in India before the beginning of the Christian era. This garment (*kañcuka*) was a constituent of the Śaka costume in Central Asia,[11] and was introduced by them in India.[12] Its earliest portrayal at Bhārhut has been described by Cunningham in detail:

There is, however, a single figure of a soldier, nearly of life size, and in such fine preservation, that all the details of his costume can be distinguished with ease. His head is bare, and the short curly hair is bound with a broad band or ribbon, which is fastened at the back of the head in a bow, with its long ends streaming in the wind. His dress consists of a tunic with long sleeves, and reaching nearly to the mid-thigh. It is tied in two places by cords; at the throat by a cord with two tassels, and across the stomach by a double-looped bow. The loins and thighs are covered with a dhotī which reaches below the knees, with the ends hanging down to the ground in front in a series of extremely stiff and formal folds. On the feet are boots, which reach high up the legs, and are either fastened or finished by a cord with two tassels, like those on the neck of the tunic.[13] (Figure 3)

SĀÑCĪ PORTRAYALS

In Sāñcī reliefs the soldiers are represented in more than one type of costume. Referring to the peculiar dress worn by archers, sitting behind the chiefs on elephants Marshall says that 'it consists of a tunic with pleated kilt (perhaps a single garment), a corded girdle or kamarband (such as chaprasis still wear) and a pullover "balaclava" cap tied with ribbons around the neck'.[14]

In another panel

it is tempting to see Yavana influence in the un-Indian attire of some of the figures in Pl. 36C 1 comprising a tunic (= Greek chiton), short cloak (= Greek chlamys), and fillet for the hair (= Greek taenia); and even the pointed, Phrygian looking caps worn by two of the figures in this relief would be appropriate to Yavanas hailing from the region of Bactria or thereabouts.[15]

Though Marshall is inclined to associate this dress with the Malla people, who came from a hill country, his observations on Yavana influence appear more convincing.

The third type of costume depicted in Sāñcī panels included *dhotī* and *kamarbandha*.[16] This suggests that indigenous and foreign dress styles remained in vogue side by side. Important items of dress depicted in Sāñcī sculptures include the following:

KILT AND TUNIC

The tunic (a short coat) and kilt appeared in India around second century BC. A war scene at Sāñcī depicts three soldiers in tunic and kilt while some others are shown bare-bodied.[17] The infantry soldiers in kilts are also depicted on the southern gateway of Sāñcī.[18] Perhaps, the tunic was introduced in India by the Greeks. Elsewhere, two *dvāra-pālas* are represented in *dhotī*. Over the *dhotī* they wear a broad belt mounted with metal plaques from which descends a skirt made up of three layers of square ended straps. Here the Roman impact is very evident.[19]

CROSS-BELTS

In many cases soldiers wear cross-belts to carry shield or quiver on the back. Cunningham has described the method of fastening the cross-belts as follows:

> The fastenings, which are apparently leather straps are passed over both shoulders, crossed in front, and carried to the back, where they were probably passed through a ring in the end of the quiver, and thus carried to the front and again crossed, the ends being secured by loops in the upper straps.[20]

TROUSERS

The appearance of trousers in India around first century BC is, however, much more significant. Originally, this dress

Plate 5: Kuṣāṇa soldier

had developed as a matter of necessity in Central Asia. 'By reason of their domestication of horse and horse-back riding the inhabitants of Central Asia were forced to discard the loose skirt like costume and to develop that ingenious piece of clothing that we call trousers. With the popularity of horse-riding it spread to other parts of the globe.'[21]

Indeed the Śakas among whom the use of long and rather wide trousers had been common since the fifth century BC,[22] introduced it in India. In the Kuṣāṇa period, it gained popularity and subsequently the Gupta kings also adopted it in imitation of the Kuṣāṇas.

FILLET

The Bhārhut warrior wears a fillet or ribbon on the head (Figure 3).[23] This was certainly a foreign importation as Indian soldiers either used a turban or went bare headed. It is remarkable that such head-scarves widely appear on the coins of Greek and Kuṣāṇa rulers.[24]

TOP BOOTS

The use of top boots was introduced in India by foreign invaders. In early art of India boots are exclusively met in association with foreigners.[25] In Mathurā art many people of possible Śaka-Kuṣāṇa lineage appear in these boots.[26] Significantly, such heavy top boots are also depicted on the coins of Kuṣāṇa rulers.[27] It was perhaps the same as *puṭṭabandha*, a shoe type referred to by Buddhaghoṣa as current among the Yavanas.[28] It is notable that the invention of boots is related to horse-back riding in Central Asia:

> Closely associated with horseback riding is another product of Central Asia, namely boots, which gradually took the place of slippers and sandals. These early boots were made either of felt or of leather, which indicates that in all probability the art of

felt-making made its way from Central Asia to other parts of the world. At a somewhat later time it was the Central Asiatics who initiated the custom of putting heels on boots and shoes.[29]

Further, the dress items, viz., coat, trousers, and boots were integral part of the the northern dress (*uddīcyaveśa*) associated with the Śaka-Kuṣāṇas.[30]

ARMOUR

The military system of a people has a direct bearing on the equipment of their soldiers. Though armour had been known to Indians since the Vedic times its wider use on Indian battlefield may be ascribed to foreign invaders. The Greeks had not seen Indian soldiers in armour in the fourth century BC. The early art of India also does not represent native soldiers in armour.[31] The soldiers depicted in armour in Indian art were indeed foreigners.[32]

The steppe people best known for heavy armour were the Sarmatians.[33] The Scythians and the Kuṣāṇas lived in their proximity for a long time before coming to India and it is, therefore, likely that they brought armour into India. The *Mahābhārata* also associates armour with foreigners like Śakas and Kambojas.[34] In the *Arthaśāstra* the *lohapaṭṭa*, and *lohajālikā* are mentioned with reference to the foreign invaders.[35]

It is notable that many Indo-Greek rulers are represented on their coins in full armour covering chest, back, and arms, and extending down to the knees.[36] Some of them are represented in breast-plate and a coat of chain-mail.[37] Kuṣāṇa king Vāsudeva appears on his coins in armour.[38] In the art of Gandhāra many soldiers are depicted in metallic armour.[39]

Some kind of armour was also meant to protect elephants and camels.[40] However, to say that 'it was certainly foreign importation as such defensive armour was unknown in early India' is far from the truth.[41]

HELMET

Indian soldiers did not use helmet in fourth century BC. In the art of Bhārhut and Sāñcī the helmet is rarely represented. The occurrence of some helmeted infantrymen in a Sāñcī[42] panel may be related to foreign invaders.

On the other hand, the helmet was common among the Indo-Greeks and their rulers are generally portrayed in helmet, variously designed and adorned.[43] The Kuṣāṇas were again very fond of helmet and many of their rulers appear with helmets on the coins.[44] Helmets are widely represented in the Kuṣāṇa art of Gandhāra.[45]

BOW

With foreign invasions some new weapons appeared in the Indian battlefield. Of these a small bow, a concomitant of the mounted archer is particularly notable. Indians had fought the battle of Jhelum with a large man-sized bow[46] and they continued its use for some more time.[47] But it was subsequently replaced by a smaller bow of Śaka-Kuṣāṇa affiliation.[48] In this connection the observations of Cunningham are significant:

> Nearly all the soldiers (at Sāñcī) are depicted as archers; but the less ancient bows are much shorter than the bearer and do not appear to have been more than four feet in length. Most of the bows appear to be straight pieces of bamboo, but a few have a double curve, with a straight hand-piece in the middle, similar to the modern ornamental bows of buffalo's horn.[49]

According to Fergusson 'their bows are bows of double flexure, which we usually associate with the Parthians or Amazons'.[50]

The most important contribution of Śaka-Kuṣāṇas to Indian weaponry was the composite bow. It was made of two curved pieces joined together by a central piece. Sarmatians and the Hūṇas were the first to use this weapon.[51] In fact, the Hūṇas striking success in overcoming neighbouring people including the Sacians and the Massagetae, was due to the use of the new extremely efficient Hunic type of bow. It was larger than the Scythic type, hitherto widespread among the steppe peoples, and was made of several pieces of different kinds of wood strengthened by bone inlays.[52]

The Śaka-Kuṣāṇas who had lived in close proximity with these people in Central Asia perhaps introduced this bow in India. The incidence of this bow in Taxila[53] could, therefore, be ascribed to the Śakas. Similar bows are represented on the coins of Indo-Parthian kings dated in second century BC.[54] The Kṣatrapas of western India continued this practice.[55]

ARROW-HEADS

The archaeological discoveries of arrow-heads also suggest foreign contribution. According to Marshall all the arrow-heads found at Taxila were intended for shafts made of reeds. Since the reed arrow was in general use among the Iranians and Central Asians as well as Indian people, it is reasonable to infer that these 'double-tanged' heads as we may call them were an adaptation of a western socketed type rather than an eastern one, and, this being so, it seems not improbable that they were introduced at Taxila by the Bactrian Greeks.[56] Around the beginning of the Christian era, i.e. Śaka-Parthian period, two new types, viz., conical and three-bladed made an appearance. The latter seems to have been favoured by the Śakas to whom its introduction at Taxila was no doubt due. This has been found along with a four-bladed type at Dharmarājika and other monasteries destroyed by the White Hūṇas in the fifth century AD. It is a reasonable surmise that the four-bladed type was used by the attacking Hūṇas and the three-bladed one, which had been introduced by the Scythians, by the defenders.[57]

Kauśāmbī has yielded three other types of arrow-heads, namely double-tanged, three-bladed and barbed-bladed.[58] These are in sharp contrast to other types discovered there. Their intrusive character is borne out by the absence of such prototypes at Kauśāmbī or elsewhere in the Gangetic valley.

Their distinctive nature, their close analogy with those from Taxilā and sudden appearance at Kauśāmbī clearly indicate that these were introduced there by the invaders from the north-west region. The Bactrian Greeks, the Śaka-Parthians and the Hūṇas, to whom Marshall ascribed these three types, are also indicated by evidence of stratigraphy at Kauśāmbī.[59]

SWORD

The foreign invaders also introduced some new sword types. These were long, double-edged and straight. In this connection the sword borne by a foreign warrior at Bhārhut is notable (Figure 3).[60] A similar sword is borne by soldiers represented at a Sāñcī gate-post.[61]

Almost similar swords are met with in the Kuṣāṇa art of India.[62] Kaniṣka himself donned a similar weapon. The Massagetan-Sacian burials of sixth and fifth centuries BC from the lower Syr Daria[63] have also yielded similar swords. The iron swords unearthed at Taxila also bear close resemblance with the sword borne by Kaniṣka in Mathurā.[64] Kuṣāṇas carried their sword in a scabbard tied to the waistband. It is said that scabbard slide originated among the nomads of Central Asia and was carried in all direction by the Yueh-chi tribe.[65] A small sword resembling the Roman gladius is also met with in the early art of Bhārhut and Sāñcī as well as in the Gandhāra reliefs.[66]

JAVELIN

Some heavy javelin types, with three or four flanged heads have been discovered at Taxila. There seems little doubt that these metal javelins were a foreign weapon introduced either by the Bactrian Greeks, or more probably by the Śakas or Parthians.[67] These are widely represented in the Kuṣāṇa art.[68] According to Rosenfield 'A giant spear as a war implement was, however, a prominent part of the armament and symbolism of the Indo-Śakas. This in itself involves basic issues of military tactics and larger cultural orientation.'[69]

SHIELD

Some shield types found in the art of Sāñcī and Gandhāra look un-Indian and were probably introduced by Śaka-Kuṣāṇas. Of these the oblong inverted type with geometrical patterns bears a close resemblance to the shield types found in the steppes.[70] This could be said with greater certainty about the round shields represented in the Gandhāra art in association with soldiers of foreign origin. The Indo-Greek kings are widely represented on their coins with a round shield.[71]

MOUNTED ARCHER

The emergence of the mounted archer on the Indian battlefield revolutionized Indian military costume, accoutrements and weaponry. Its earliest representation is met on the coins of the Pahlava rulers of north-west India.[72] But it were the Śaka-Kuṣāṇas who popularized this mode of warfare. The costume and accoutrement of the archers represented in Harwan tiles (Kashmir) suggest definite Central Asian connection.[73] However, the art of mounted archery did not strike deep roots in Indian soil. Introduced by the Parthians and continuing for some time as a sickly exotic, it withered away shortly after the Gupta period. This is the impression that one gathers from a study of records of post-Gupta India.[74]

ACCOUTREMENTS OF HORSE

With the mounted archer some new accoutrements for horse also appeared. The earliest evidence of the stirrup in India is met in the art of Sāñcī.[75] According to Marshall this is the earliest example by some five centuries of the use of the stirrup in any part of the world.[76] Subsequently, it is also met with at Mathurā.[77] Stirrup is also depicted on some coins,[78] suggesting that it was a Śaka-Kuṣāṇa contribution.[79]

Indians did not use a proper saddle in fourth century BC.[80] But for a mounted archer the saddle was a necessity. In Sāñcī sculptures the only saddle appears in association with a rider of foreign origin,[81] perhaps a Scythian. In the Kuṣāṇa art of Gandhāra, the saddles are widely represented.[82]

Indians did not use curved bit in fourth century BC. Its representation in the art of Sāñcī,[83] however, suggests that it was introduced in India by foreigners like Indo-Greeks or Scythians. The discovery of snaffle bits from Taxila also confirms this. The cheek bars of the bridle are either 'S' shaped with two holes for rein-strap or having slight curves.[84]

The invaders also used some kind of horse armour is evident from excavations at Taxila.[85] The *Arthaśāstra* says that in the *śuddha aśva vyūha* (unmixed horse array) the armoured horses were to be deployed in the wings and flanks to launch attack.[86]

DECLINE OF CHARIOT

Chariot, horse and elephant were the three vehicles of war in fourth century BC. Of these the chariot just failed to measure up to the fast moving cavalry of the invaders and soon faded out of the Indian battlefield. According to Macdonell, 'the use of chariot both for war and for racing gradually died out in Hindustan, partly perhaps owing to the unnerving influence of the climate and partly to the scarcity of horses, which had to be brought from the region of the Indus'.[87] In this context the opinion of Wilson is also significant.

> As with the Greeks so with the Hindus the horse came to supersede the chariot. There is no mention of the latter in the accounts given by Mohammedan writers of their first engagement with the Hindus. Its use is characteristic of antiquity and its exchange for the horse may probably be ascribed in some degree to the infusion of Scythian tribes and manners from the west about the commencement of our era.[88]

This survey of military costume and accoutrements during the Śaka-Kuṣāṇa period testifies that striking changes had taken place. The native soldiers adopted, alien systems of dressing, weaponry and even strategy and tactics from the invaders. Some sort of dress synthesis is very much evident in the art of Kuṣāṇas. The invaders introduced a new type of costume which included coat, trousers, boots and helmet. It is notable that the nature of this costume is anatomical as against the indigenous type which is gravitational. They also introduced a long sword, a giant spear and a short bow convenient for mounted archers.

Perhaps, they were the people who introduced saddle, curved bit, and stirrup for a better use of the horse in the battlefield.

NOTES

1. J.M. Rosenfield, *Dynastic Art of the Kushāṇs*, p. 55.
2. Ibid., p. 125; also coins 272, 278, 279.
3. H. Ingholt, *Gandhāran Art in Pakistan*, pl. 561, p. 193.
4. Ibid., pl. 64; also pls. 47, 63.
5. Rosenfield, op. cit., p. 102.
6. Ibid., p. 54, coins 30, 31.
7. A.H. Longhurst, *The Budhist Antiquities of Nāgārjunīkoṇḍa*, pp. 11, 24.
8. R.B. Whitehead, *Catalogue of the Coins in the Punjab Museum*, pl. 17.36.
9. L. Bachhofer, *Early Indian Sculpture*, pl. 76.
10. J.W. M'Crindle, *Ancient India as Described by Megasthenese and Arrian*, p. 219.
11. W.M. McGovern, *Early Empires of Central Asia*, pl. 1.
12. Moti Chandra, *Prācīna Bhāratīya Veśa-bhūṣā*, pp. 142-3.
13. A. Cunningham, *The Stūpa of Bhārhut*, p. 32.
14. Marshall and Foucher, *The Monuments of Sāñchī*, pl. 15.3; also vol. 1, p. 119. fn. 1.
15. Ibid., pl. 36c, p. 157 fn. 1.
16. Ibid., pl. 15.3.
17. Ibid.
18. Ibid.
19. M.N. Deshpande, *Ancient India*, no. 15, pl. 51 A and B.
20. A. Cunningham, *The Bhilsā Topes*, p. 138.
21. McGovern, op. cit., p. 2.
22. E. Herzfeld, *MASI*, no. 38, p. 5.
23. Cunningham, *The Stūpa of Bhārhut*, p. 32, pl. 32.4.
24. Whitehead, op. cit., vol. 1, pls. 8.610, 616-17; 16.96, 100, 109, etc.
25. Cunningham, op. cit. pl. 32.4; Rosenfield, op. cit., pls. 1, 2, 13, 22, 24, etc.
26. In Mathurā art Kuṣāṇa rulers are represented in these shoes.

27. P. Gardner, *The Coins of Greeks and Scythic Kings of Bactria and India in the British Museum*, pls. 25.7, etc.
28. Moti Chandra, op. cit., p. 39.
29. McGovern, op. cit., p. 2.
30. U.P. Thapliyal, *Foreign Elements in Ancient Indian Society*, p. 150.
31. R. Russell's (*Oriental Armour*, p. 89) observation that 'as far as you can judge the Indians were without defensive armour except the shield which for many centuries is the only protection shown in Hindu sculptures' is, therefore, partially true.
32. A. Foucher, *L'Art Greco Bouddique Du Gandhāra*, Figs. 202, 204, 292; also R. Russel, Oriental Armour, p. 89.
33. T. Sulimirski, *The Sarmatians*, pp. 31-2.
34. *Mbh*, Droṇa, 95, 39-45.
35. *Arthaśāstra*, 2.18.16.
36. Whitehead, op. cit., pls. 4.229, 6.515, 7.599, 8.610.
37. Ibid., pls. 1.27, 2.64, 7.577.
38. Ibid., pls. 19.236, also 209, 210, 211, etc.
39. Ingholt, op. cit., pls. 63, 64, etc.
40. J. Marshall, *Taxila*, p. 549.
41. Ibid., p. 208; also A.L. Basham, *The Wonder That Was India*, p. 133.
42. Marshall and Foucher, op. cit. (southern gateway) pls.
43. Whitehead, op. cit., pls. 2-9; also A.N. Lahiri, *Corpus of Indo-Greek Coins*, pp. 23-4.
44. Ibid., pls. 17-20; also see Rosenfield, op. cit., fig. 6.
45. Foucher, op. cit., p. 95, fig. 253, p. 97, fig. 354; On their coins Kuṣāṇa rulers are represented in as many as 7 helmet types. Rosenfield, op. cit., p. 67, fig. 6.
46. J.W. M'Crindle, *Ancient India*, p. 220.
47. Bhārhut and Sāñcī furnish such specimens.
48. The Scythians used a double curved bow made of horn and strung with sinews both for hunting and warfare. Their arrows had trefoil shaped heads ... bows and arrows were carried in a combined case known as *gorytus* which was worn slung from the belt at the left hip. T.T. Rice, *The Scythians*, p. 75.
49. Cunningham, *The Bhilsā Topes*, p. 139.
50. J. Fergusson, *Tree and Serpent Worship*, p. 138.
51. Sulimirsky, op. cit., fig. 4, p. 28.
52. Ibid., pp. 113-14.

53. G.S. Ghurye, *Indian Costume*, fig. 49.
54. H.C. Raychaudhuri, *Political History of Ancient India*, p. 484.
55. Ibid.
56. Marshall, *Taxila*, p. 547.
57. Ibid., p. 548.
58. G.R. Sharma, *Excavations at Kauśāmbī*, p. 46.
59. Ibid.
60. Cunningham, *The Stūpa of Bhārhut*, pp. 32-3.
61. P.S. Rawson, *The Indian Sword*, p. 16.
62. Rosenfield, op. cit., pls. 2, 2a; Coin nos. 205, 217, 218, 241; also Cunningham, *The Stūpa of Bhārhut*, pl. 32.
63. Sulimirski, op. cit., fig. 17.
64. Marshall, *Taxila*, p. 545, pl. 164; also Rawson, op. cit., pp. 6-7.
65. Rosenfield, op. cit., p. 179.
66. Marshall, *Taxila*, p. 545; also Rawson, op. cit., p. 18.
67. Marshall, ibid., p. 546.
68. Foucher, op. cit., Figs. 31, 149, 181, 280, 288, etc.
69. Rosenfield, op. cit., p. 55.
70. Hallade, op. cit., pls.
71. Lahiri, op. cit., pls. 24.9, 10, 13; 25.6-7; 12.7.
72. V.A. Smith, *Coins of Ancient India: Catalogue of the Coins in the Indian Museum Calcutta*, p. 43, pl. 9.7.
73. R.C. Kak, *Ancient Monuments of Kashmir*, pls. 23.3, 28.14, etc.
74. P.C. Chakravarti, *The Art of War in Ancient India*, p. 42.
75. F.C. Maisey, *Sāñchī and its Remains*, pls. 7, 26.
76. J. Marshall, *A Guide to Sāñchī*, p. 152, fn. 3.
77. V.A. Smith, *The Jain Stūpa and other Antiquities of Mathurā*, pl. 15.
78. P. Gardner, *A Catalogue of Indian Coins in the British Museum*, pls. 14.7, 13.
79. According to Kanchan Chakravarty the occurrence of stirrup in the sculptures of Bhāja, Sāñcī, and Mathurā speak of a Irano-Hellenistic infiltration and gradual assimilation. *Society, Religion, and Art in Kuṣāṇa Period*, p. 102.
80. M'Crindle, *Ancient India*, p. 221.
81. Marshall and Foucher, op. cit., p. 97.
82. Ingholt, op. cit., pls. 49, 51.
83. Saddle is represented only once at Sāñcī.

84. Marshall, *Taxila*, pp. 171, 176, 193, 208, 550-1, pls. 96-8, 165 etc.
85. Ibid., p. 549.
86. *Arthaśāstra*, 10.5.34-7.
87. A.A. Macdonell, *A History of Sanskrit Literature*, p. 168.
88. H.H. Wilson, *Collected Works*, vol. 4, p. 297.

CHAPTER 8

Gupta Age and After

The Gupta dynasty ruled in India from fourth to sixth century AD. Its rulers built a strong army which earned them numerous victories. In all probability the Gupta army was equipped by the state on the Mauryan pattern. A reasonably true picture of Gupta soldier can be formed by piecing together art and literary evidence.

SYNTHESIS

The military costume and accoutrements of the Gupta age were an amalgam of Maurya-Śuṅga and Śaka-Kuṣāṇa traditions. This is best illustrated by the coin issues of the Gupta kings, as they appear dressed in native as well as foreign costume comprising tunic and trousers. According to A.S. Altekar:

> The convenience and also the elegant cut of sewn garments must have appealed to the highly artistic but practical commonsense of the Guptas. This commonsense in the sphere of dress is also reflected in changing from heavy woollen material of the Kuṣāṇa costume to thin and at times diaphanous material, which suited well with the climatic conditions of the Gangetic plain. The coarseness and heavy barbaric cut of the Kuṣāṇa garments gave place to elegance and finish. Now, the top boots of the Kuṣāṇas also lost their heaviness and were reduced to the shape of modern riding boots.[1]

Gupta rulers generally appear on their coins in full boots decorated with buttons; trousers, churidars, pleated or salwar type; tunic or coats with or without pointed ends; caps and helmets (Figure 12).[2] These dress items were indeed borrowed by them from the Kuṣāṇas. But it was not one way traffic as the foreigners also borrowed Indian military ethos, costume, etc. The army of Śaka Mahākṣatrapa Rudradāman is stated to have comprised four arms (*caturaṅgiṇī*) though the army of invading Śakas could not have included chariots and elephants in the beginning. Further, in Gandhāra sculptures many foreign warriors donning armour also wear Indian *dhotī*.[3]

EVIDENCE OF BĀṆA BHAṬṬA

A detailed description of military costume of this period is met in the *Harṣacarita* of Bāṇa Bhaṭṭa. It says that before the marching entourage of prince Dadhīca,

> ran an army of foot about a thousand strong, mostly young men, with clusters of crisp hanging hair upon their foreheads, and cheeks laughing with the bright gleam of their ear ornaments; girt with scented jerkins spotted with a powder of black aloe wood paste; their upper garment formed into turbans; sparkling golden bracelets on their left forearms, daggers fastened in strong knots in their sashes of doubled cloth.... Clubs at their sides, swords in their hands.[4]

Referring to the lower garment of Dadhīca, Bāṇa says that 'his slim waist was marked off by a tight drawn lower garment of *harita* green (pigeon green), of which one corner was gracefully set in front a little below the navel and the hem hung over the girdle behind, and which on both sides was so girt up as to display a third of his thigh'.[5] In this description the occurrence of *kañcuka*[6] and *śiroveṣṭana*[7] is significant.

Bāṇa also describes the costume of the chieftains of Harṣa who had come to join battle, mounted on elephants.

Figure 12: Gupta king in military costume

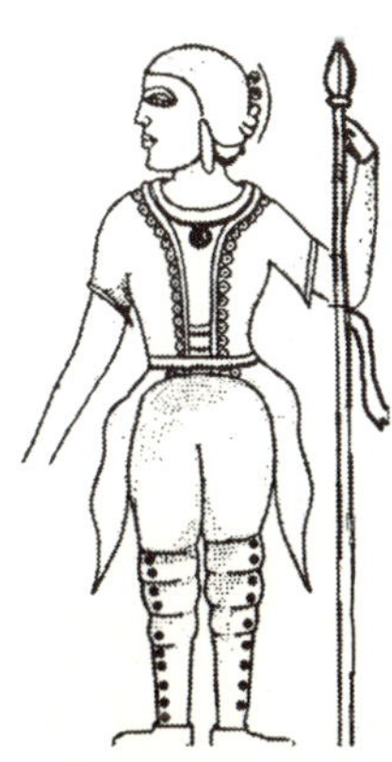

The clash of their swaying foot-rest augmented the sound from the precious stones in their anklets. Their shanks were covered with their proper covering of delicate tinted silk. Their copper coloured legs were chequerred with mud stained wraps, and a heightened white was produced by contrast with trousers soft and dark as bees. They wore tunics darkened by black diamonds glistering on bright forms; Chinese cuirasses were thrown over them; coats used double showing clusters of bright pearls, bodices speckled with a mixture of various colours, and shawls of the shade of parrots' tails. Fine waistbands were wound about flanks made thin by exercise. Servants ran up to loose dangling ear-rings which had become entangled with pearl necklaces, tossed by their movements; Their heads were wrapt in shawls of a soft saffron hue. They had linen turbans inlaid with bits of crest jems.[8]

Their turbans covered the upper part of the ears. They carried shields of various colours.[9]

HEADDRESS

It seems that the turban went out of fashion during the early centuries of Christian era. Perhaps, a wider use of helmet as a result of foreign impact made it redundant. Meanwhile, a hair-band had come into vogue to tie up the hair. It was a common wear with the Persians and Scythians[10] and a warrior, most probably a foreigner, represented in the Bhārhut art actually dons a hair-band.[11]

That during the Gupta age the soldiers widely used hair-bands is evident from the Ajantā paintings (Figures 13, 14).[12] In the *Harṣacarita* the royal bodyguard Mekhalaka and the royal messenger Kuraṅgaka are also described as wearing hair-bands (*cīra*).[13]

The helmet, introduced by the Śaka-Kuṣāṇas continued but now its use was mostly restricted to the rulers and commanders. Many Gupta rulers are represented donning a helmet on their coins (Figure 12).[14] In Ajantā paintings

Plate 6: Gupta soldier

Figure 13: Elephants on the march, Ajantā

Figure 14: Army on the march, Ajantā

some soldiers also wear a similar helmet.[15] However, the soldiers in general wore some kind of Indian turban or a fillet.[16]

UPPER GARMENT

For the upper garment soldiers used a short length half-sleeved garment called *kūrpāsa* as borne out by art[17] and literary evidence.[18] But the rulers and senior commanders used long coats or cut-tailed coats.[19] The *Harṣacarita* refers to four coat types, viz., *cīna-colaka*, *vārabāṇa*, *kañcuka* and *kūrpāsaka* in relation to soldiers and high dignitaries.[20] These coat types, introduced by the Śaka-Kuṣāṇas, remained in use during the Gupta age in a modified form, suitable for the Indian climatic conditions.

This is amply borne out by the Gupta coins as also the Ajantā art. In the new evolved form the coat appears elegantly stitched out of some light or diaphanous fabric.[21] It is designed in full sleeves or half sleeves and in full length or half length depending upon the taste of the bearer.[22] Generally, the coats appear heavily embroidered, with rows of beads or buttons adorning the front, neck and sleeves.[23] The Gupta soldiers may have used similar coats, with little adornments.

LOWER GARMENT

For the lower garment soldiers used an *ardhoruka*[24] or *caṇḍātaka* (skirt) (Figures 13, 14, 15).[25] The horsemen preferred the latter as it was convenient in mounting.[26] The trousers are not widely represented in the Ajantā art because these were used by kings and commanders only.[27] The Gupta rulers are often represented in trousers, adorned with buttons along the seams, on their coins.[28] There are minor variations in the make of the trousers in designing but the best one very closely resemble the modern riding breeches.[29] The *Harṣacarita* has mentioned three trousers types, viz., *svasthāna*, *piṅgā*, and *satulā*, as the dress of kings and commanders.[30] These types have been explained as long length, short length and very short length respectively.[31]

Despite the use of trousers by kings and commanders the *dhotī* continued as the most popular lower garment among natives, the soldiers and civilians alike, as is evident from coins and Ajantā paintings.[32] Gupta rulers appear in a *dhotī* wrapped in different styles.[33] Bāṇa Bhaṭṭa has given a detailed description of the lower garment or *dhotī* worn by Dadhīca in the *Harṣacarita*:[34]

1. It was tied tightly around the waist.
2. One of the end projected on the front side just below the naval.

Figure 15: Soldiers in action, Ajantā

3. Another end of the garment was tucked behind in such a manner that a part of it projected upward.
4. When the body was bent forward the garment left a part of the thigh exposed.
5. The garment was green in colour like a *hārīta* bird.

WAIST-BAND

The waist-band continued to be a part of the soldier's costume during the Gupta age,[35] but now its shape was unlike the Maurya-Śuṅga band of intertwined cords. The Gupta waist-band appears more as an adornment than a necessary adjunct to the soldier's costume. It also formed a part of *uddīcyaveśa* (northern dress) of the Śaka-Kuṣāṇa invaders.[36] The *Harṣacarita* describes the kings and commanders as wearing attractive sashes.[37]

FOOTWEAR

Indians had been using some kind of footwear since the Vedic times, but the foreigners contributed in popularizing boots in India. In the art of Ajantā soldiers generally appear in sandals with straps tied around the ankles,[38] similar to the Greco-Roman sandals, and may well have been introduced by the Indo-Greeks. But the rulers and military commanders used top boots, is evident from Gupta coins.[39] In this connection the observations of Altekar are significant:

> usually the kings on Gupta coins are shown wearing full boots decorated with buttons. On the authority of the *Bṛhatkalpasūtra-bhāṣya* these boots could be identified with *khallaka*, *ardha-khallaka*, *khapusā* and *jaṅghā* types. The *ardha-khallakā* type covered half the leg, the *samasta-khallaka* covered the full leg; the *khapusā* covered the knees and *jaṅghā* and *ardha-jaṅghā* covered either full or half thighs. Apparently these shoes had fasteners. They were sewn or even fastened with, two, three or more lines of sewing or fastening.[40]

Kuṣāṇa influence is very much evident here. In this connection it is notable that the various types of boots represented on Gupta coins are less heavy and better designed than the heavy top boots of the Kuṣāṇas. In fact, these are much akin to modern horse-riding boots.

APRON (*ĀCCHĀDANAKA*)

While marching to the battlefield the high ranking commanders put on an apron.[41] It was a sheet of cloth, which was thrown over the shoulders, with two ends tied on the chest in front. In some Mathurā sculptures Sūrya and his descendants are represented with apron, suggesting that it was a part of the Sassanian costume.[42] In the Ajantā art some soldiers don an apron.[43] Though apron had come into vogue around the beginning of the Christian era,[44] it became popular during the Gupta age only.

ARMOUR

The body armour introduced by the Śaka-Kuṣāṇas may have continued during the Gupta period.[45] A sculpture from Nāgārjunīkoṇḍa dated to third or fourth century AD represents a bearded Scythian soldier in a helmet, a quilted full-sleeved coat, and tight fitting trousers.[46] Another sculpture represents a horse-rider wearing a long-sleeved tunic over tight-fitting trousers. It also depicts a foot-soldier in a long-sleeved and round-necked coat and a helmet.[47] Perhaps, the long and quilted coat had become a substitute for the earlier armour in the Gupta age. A warrior thus dressed up was called *sannadha*, *varmita*, *sajja*, *danśita* or *vyūḍa-kaṅkaṭa*.[48]

WEAPONS

All soldiers carried some kind of weapon. According to Xuan Zang:

the infantry go lightly into action and are choice men of valour; They bear a large shield and carry a long spear; some are armed with a sword or saber and dash to the front of the advancing line of battle. They are perfect experts with all the implements of war such as spear, shield, bow and arrow, sword, saber, and having been drilled in them for generations.[49]

Bow

The bow continued to enjoy superiority over all other arms during the Gupta age. The art, literary and numismatic evidence confirms the use of three types of bows, viz., single-curved, double-curved, and composite. The single curved, widely met in the art of Ajantā, was probably used by hunters and foot-soldiers.[50] The double curved bow was longer than the single curved one and was generally borne by higher dignitaries.[51] The composite bow had been introduced by the Scythians,[52] and was the favourite weapon of Gupta kings.[53] It is widely represented in the Ajantā art.[54]

The bow-man always carried a quiver on the back. It was fastened with two straps—the upper strap was carried over from the left shoulder and passed below the right arm and the lower strap was tied round the chest.[55] Occasionally, a warrior (bow-man) was accompanied by an arrow-bearer called *kāṇḍavat* or *kāṇḍira.*[56]

Sword

The sword made of iron or steel, curved or straight, was another popular weapon of the Gupta age. It is said that during the Gupta period the old indigenous leaf bladed sword, which was popular during the Scytho-Kuṣāṇa period, underwent some changes and attained a form very close to that of a modern *khaṇḍā.* This suggests remarkable

2. The eyes were covered with a cloth, which was removed at the commencement of the battle.[67]

A goad called *aṅkuśa* or *śṛṇi* was used to command the elephant.[68] In elephant-rider type coins King Kumaragupta I is depicted with a goad in right hand.[69] The elephant was also driven with a whip called *totra* or *vaiṇuka.*[70] Quivers filled with arrows were tied to the howdah.[71]

Upholstering of an elephant is described in some detail in the *Avantisundarīkathā* of Daṇḍin. Though it is a later work, the details furnished by it may hold true in respect of the Gupta age.

Their temples were thickly anointed with vermilion paste; ears were adorned with white conches and chowries that overhung them; tusks were plated with gold or iron; flank was tied with girths (*kakṣya*) and neck with chain; the mouth was covered with a piece of red cloth and the back was overlaid with a sheet of leather (*vṛṣi*) of reddish hue and on it was placed the golden saddle (*paryāṇaka*) with jewels hanging on all sides of it, overspread with variegated blankets and cushions with their scabbard embroidered with gold thread.[72]

The stair-like convenience which enabled the rider to climb up to the seat was called *kalpanā* or *sajjanā.*[73]

Horse

The equipment of the horse generally included bridle (*khalina*), thorny bridle (*kharakhalina*), stirrup (*ūruvadhra*), seat or saddle (*paryāṇa*), collars (*graiveya*), girth (*kakṣya*), leather covering for eyes (*pakṣacarman*) and iron soles on the hooves (*maṇḍūra*).[74] Rings on the forehead, necklace, whisk-strings and bell-strings also formed a part of its adornment.[75]

There is some confusion about the use of saddle during the Gupta age. In Gupta coins and Ajantā paintings saddles are well represented[76] but Alberuni (eleventh century) has said that Indians did not use a saddle.[77] Chakravarty opines that

> the only way in which we can harmonise these two rival sets of evidence is on the supposition that though the use of the saddle was well known in the country, the mass of the people rode their horses without one. It is possible that the use of saddle was regarded as a mark of distinction, and was consequently confined to the higher aristocratic classes.[78]

A quiver was also tied to the saddle.[79]

The saddle was adorned with accessories like *lavaṇa-kalāyī*. These were made of small pieces of wood, cast into deer models, and hung on the saddle. Such adornments of horse are widely met with in the Gupta coins and the art of Amarāvatī.[80] The saddle cloth depicted on Gupta coins is patterned in flowery designs. The edges of the cloth were decorated with strings of beads or pearls.[81] Gupta coins are a sure guide to the complete adornments of horse during this period.[82]

It seems that the stirrup had come into vogue by the Gupta age. On some Gupta coins, stirrup is clearly depicted.[83] In the *Harṣacarita* there is a clear mention of stirrup (*pādafalikā*).[84] Bits were used but horses without bits were also known. In Ajantā cave XVII (fourth century AD) horses are represented wearing bits, but in cave I they appear without a bit. It seems that the old tradition of 'guiding the horse, with or without bit, continued side by side for centuries'.[85]

The practice of fixing iron-soles (*maṇḍūra*) to the hooves of horse may have started during the Gupta age. In the *Amarakośa maṇḍūra* is stated to be an object of iron.[86] But Daṇḍin uses the term in the actual sense of iron-sole.[87] This goes against the generally held view that the iron soles for the horses (*nālabandī*) were introduced in India by the Turk invaders.[88]

In this context it is notable that the chariot had nearly faded out of Indian battlefields at the dawn of the Gupta dynasty. However, the chariots continued to be depicted widely in the war scenes portrayed in the temples for a long time. In the temples at Belur and Helebid the warriors are often depicted mounted on chariots. A terracotta plaque discovered from Ahicchatra also depicts two chariot warriors confronting each other (Figure 16). Further, in the later works like *Raghuvaṁśa, Siśupālavadha* and *Naiṣadhacarita*. The chariot is widely mentioned as a valuable component of the army.

PURĀṆIC VIEW

In the Purāṇas there are some interesting references to the military costume worn by the gods and demons when engaged in war. The *Matsya Purāṇa* says that the look of the army of the demons in blue costume was comparable to the sky full of blue clouds and that of the gods in white and black costume with stars, moon and sun.[89]

The *Brahmāṇḍa Purāṇa* also furnishes some useful information in this regard. When the Daitya army led by Visaṅga dressed for war, the generals put on dark-coloured turbans. All their equipment was dark coloured and they appeared to have become one with dense darkness. Visaṅga put on round his chest the armour named *meghadombaraka*. His dress and accoutrements were fitted with the nocturnal battle. In the same manner, his entire army too had dark-coloured armour and other equipment.[90]

The *Bhāgavata Purāṇa* also supplies some sketchy information on the dress of the soldiers:

Like two oceans swarming with sea monsters shone the two (warring) armies of Deva and Dānava warriors with their ranks of fighters distinguished by their flags of different colours, by their spotless white umbrellas... their upper garments and

Figure 16: Chariot warriors. Ahicchatra

turbans waved up by winds and with their burnished armours and ornaments glittering brightly and their sharp weapons sparkling in the rays of sun.[91]

A survey of the military costume in the Gupta age leads to the conclusion that it was greatly influenced by the Śaka-Kuṣāṇa model. The Gupta kings donned the Kuṣāṇa royal dress comprising a close fitting coat (*cugha*), trousers creased at knees, high boots, close fitting cap and helmet. The soldiers in general appear to have followed their masters in imbibing the new dress style. However, some soldiers continued with the reformed traditional Indian costume. *Dhotī* was now gird more smartly and the loose ends were tied up. The *uttarīya* was replaced by *kūrpāsa* or short jacket. The head was covered with a helmet and a hair-band was widely used to tie up the hair (Figure 15).

NOTES

1. A.S. Altekar, *Catalogue of the Gupta Gold Coins in the Bayana Hoard*, p. clii.
2. Ibid., see pls.
3. H. Ingholt, *Gandhāran Art in Pakistan*, pls.
4. *Harṣacarita* (Cowell), p. 16.
5. Ibid., p. 18.
6. कृष्णशबलकाषायकंचुकेन। *Harṣacarita*, p. 21.
7. उत्तरीयकृतशिरोवेष्टनेन। Ibid.
8. Ibid., pp. 202-3.
9. Ibid., p. 203.
10. U.P. Thapliyal, *Foreign Elements in Ancient Indian Society*, p. 56.
11. A. Cunningham, *The Stūpa of Bhārhut*, pl. 32.1.
12. G. Yazdani, *Ajantā*, vol. 4, pls. 28, etc.; Maurya-Śuṅga type of turbans are met only in the paintings of cave 9. See J. Griffiths, *The Paintings in the Buddhist Cave Temples of Ajantā*, pl. 37.
13. *Harṣacarita*, pp. 52, 151.
14. A.S. Altekar, *The Coinage of the Gupta Empire*, pls. 1, 2, 3, etc.

15. Yazdani, op. cit., pls. 11(a), 12(d) also 27 (c) and 28.
16. *Harṣacarita*, pp. 202-3.
17. Yazdani, op. cit., pl. 21 (a) (b); pl. 60 (a) (b).
18. नानाकाषायकर्बुरकूर्पासकैः। *Harṣacarita*, p. 206.
19. Yazdani, op. cit., Pls. 10, 16, 18, 31, 34 (B); Griffiths, op. cit., pl. 33.
20. कञ्चुकैश्चोपचितचीनचोलकैश्च तारामुक्तास्तबकितस्तवरक वारबाणैश्च। *Harṣa-carita*, p. 206; also *Amarakośa*, 2.8.63.
21. Altekar, *Catalogue of the Gupta Gold Coins in the Bayana Hoard*, pls. 24-7.
22. Ibid., pls. 16-19.
23. Ibid., pls. 8.10, 10.5, etc.
24. G. Yazdani, op. cit., pl. 60 (a) (b).
25. Ibid.
26. Ibid.
27. Ibid., pl. 68 (b) (c).
28. Altekar, *The Coinage of the Gupta Empire*, pls.
29. Ibid.
30. उच्चित्रनेत्रसुकुमारस्वस्थगनस्थगितजङ्घाकाण्डैश्च कार्दमिकपटकल्माषितपिशङ्ग पिङ्गैः अलिनीलमसृणसतुलासमुत्पादितसितसमायोगपरभागैश्च। *Harṣacarita*, p. 206.
31. स्वस्थानं स्वस्थानेति यस्याः प्रसिद्धिः। पिङ्गा जङ्घिका।
सतुला अर्धजङ्घिका इत्यन्ये। Ibid., p. 206 (Sankara's note).
32. Yazdani, op. cit., pls. 28, 31 (B).
33. Altekar, *Catalogue of the Gupta Gold Coins in the Bayana Hoard*, pls. 5.13; 6.3, 10; 8.11; 10.13; 16.10, etc.
34. पुरस्तादीषदधोनाभिनिहितैककोणकमनीयेन पृष्ठतः कक्ष्याधिकक्षिप्तपल्लवेनोभयतः संवलनप्रकटितोरुत्रिभागेन हारीतहरिता निबिडनिपीडितेनाधरवाससा विभज्यमानत-नुतरमध्यभागम्। *Harṣacasita*, p. 22
35. Altekar, *Catalogue of the Gupta Gold Coins in the Bayana Hoard*, pls. 12,14.
36. V.S. Agrawala, *Harṣacarita Eka Sāṁskṛtika Adhyayana*, p. 154.
37. चारुशस्त्रैश्च। *Harṣacarita*, p. 207; but soldiers generally wore a waist-band in double-fold, tied at the centre. द्विगुणपट्टपट्टिकागाढ-ग्रन्थितासिधेनुना। *Harṣacarita*, p. 21.
38. Yazdani, op. cit., pls. 4(c), 29(b).
39. Altekar, *Catalogue of the Gupta Gold Coins in the Bayana Hoard*, pls.

40. Ibid., p. cliv.
41. *Harṣacarita*, p. 206.
42. Agrawala, op. cit., p. 153.
43. Yazdani, op. cit., vol. 4, pl. 37 (b), vol. 2, pl. 14.
44. F.C. Maisey, *Sāñchī and its Remains*, pl. 27.
45. The representation of armour on Gupta coins and in Ajantā art is rare.
46. A. Longhurst, *The Buddhist Antiquities of Nāgārjunīkoṇḍa, Madras Presidency*, MASI, pl. 10c, 33.6.
47. Ibid.
48. *Amarakośa*, 2.8.65.
49. T. Watters, *On Yuan Chwang's Travels in India*, vol. 1, p. 171.
50. Yazdani, op. cit., pl. 12 (d).
51. Ibid., vol. 4, pl. 37 (b); Griffiths, op. cit., pl. 83.
52. P.K. Gode, *Studies in Indian Cultural History*, vol. II, pp. 57-8.
53. Altekar, *Catalogue of the Gupta Gold Coins in the Bayana Hoard*, pls.
54. Griffiths, op. cit., p. 15, fig. 40.
55. Yazdani, op. cit., pl. 68 (a).
56. *Amarakośa*, 2.8.69.
57. P.S. Rawson, *Thc Indian Sword*, p. 22.
58. Yazdani, op. cit., pl. 37 (b); *Amarakośa*, uses the word खड्गपिधान for sheath.
59. Altekar, *Catalogue of the Gupta Gold Coins in the Bayāna Hoard*, pl. 9.15-17.
60. Griffiths, op. cit., p. 14, fig. 33.
61. Ibid.
62. K.De. B. Codrington, *IA*, vol. 59, 1930, p. 170.
63. M.K. Dhavalikar, *Ajantā: A Cultural Study*, pl. 28.13; also रुचिरकांचनपत्रभंगभंगुराणामतिबन्धुपरिवेशानां कार्दरंगचर्मणां संभारान् । *Harṣacarita*, p. 207 (Śaṅkara).
64. Agrawala, op. cit., pp. 156, 168.
65. *Harṣacarita* (Cowell), p. 202; दूष्या and वरत्रा were two other names of कक्ष्या. *Amarakośa*, 2.8.42.
66. Watters, op. cit., vol. 1, p. 171; also *Viṣṇu Dh. Pu.*, 2.177.48.
67. *Śiśupālavadha*, 18, 28-30.
68. अंकुशोऽस्त्री सृणि । *Amarakośa*, 2.8.41.
69. Altekar, *Catalogue of Gupta Gold Coins in the Bayana Hoard*, pl. 31.1-3.
70. *Amarakośa*, 2.8.41.

71. Yazdani, op. cit., pl. 55, also 54(a).
72. D.R. Gupta, *Society and Culture in the time of Daṇḍin*, p. 175; The cloth overlaid on the back of the elephant was called प्रवेणी, आस्तरण, वर्ण, परिस्तोम and कुथ. *Amarakośa*, 2.8.42. The adornments of elephant also included ध्वजपटपटुपटहशंखचामराङ्गराग-रमणीयै:। *Harṣacarita*, p. 58.
73. *Amarakośa*, 2.8.42.
74. Gupta, op. cit., p. 180.
75. Ibid.; also see *Harṣacarita*, p. 23; *Amarakośa*, 2.8.44-50.
76. Yazdani, op. cit., pl. 34; Yazdani says that 'inside the stables saddles may be noticed placed on pegs fixed into the wall. The saddles in their shape do not differ much from the saddles of the present day.' Ibid., vol. 4, p. 60; also Griffiths, op. cit., pl. 77; *Harṣacarita* also refers to the use of saddle, p. 206 (Śaṅkara).
77. E.C. Sacau, *Alberuni's India*, vol. 1, p. 181.
78. P.C. Chakravarti, *The Art of War in Ancient India*, p. 40.
79. Yazdani, op. cit., pl. 45 (b).
80. Agrawala, op. cit., p. 143.
81. Altekar, *Catalogue of the Gupta Gold Coins in the Bayana Hoard*, pls. 13.8, 22.8-15.
82. Ibid., pls.
83. Ibid., p. 241, pl. 14.7, 13.
84. प्रचलपादफलिका:। *Harṣacarita*, p. 206. It seems that the term उरवध्र was also used for stirrup. उरवध्रारोपितचरणयुगल। *Harṣacarita*, p. 31.
85. Chakravarti, op. cit., p. 39.
86. *Amarakośa*, 2.9.98.
87. Gupta, op. cit., p. 175.
88. A.J. Qaisar, subscribes to this view and says that *nālabandī* gave the invaders a definite edge over their Hindu opponents (article in *Indian Journal of History of Science*).
89. सा दीप्तशस्त्रप्रवरा दैत्यानां रुरुचे चमू:।।
    द्यौर्निमीलितसर्वाङ्गा घना नीलाम्बुदागमे
    देवतानामपि चमूर्मुमुदे शक्रपालिता।।
    उपेता सितकृष्णाभ्यां ताराभ्यां चन्द्रसूर्ययो:। *Matsya Purāṇa*, 176.15-17.
90. *Brahmāṇḍa Purāṇa*, 25.42.50.
91. *Bhāgavata Purāṇa*, 8.10.13-15.

Bibliography

ORIGINAL SOURCES

Ṛgveda Saṁhitā, ed. and tr. S.D. Satvalekar, Swadhyaya Mandal, Paradi, 1978.

———, English tr. Ralph T.H. Griffith, Motilal Banarsidass, Delhi, 1973.

Atharvaveda Saṁhitā, ed. and tr. S.D. Satvalekar, Swadhyaya Mandal, Paradi, 1985

———, English tr. W.T. Whitney, Motilal Banarsidass, Delhi, 1962.

Aitareya Brāhmaṇa, English tr. M. Haug, Bharatiya Publishing Home, Delhi, 1976.

Śatapatha Brāhmaṇa, ed. and tr. G.P. Upadhyaya, N. Delhi, 1967.

Taittirīya Saṁhitā, ed. T.N. Dharmadhikari, Vaidika Samsodhana Mandal, Poona, 1981.

Aṣṭādhyāyī, ed. and tr. S.C. Basu, Motilal Banarsidass, Delhi, 1962.

Śukla Yajurveda Saṁhitā, ed. V.L. Pansikar, Nirnaya Sagar Press, Bombay, 1912.

Samvidhāna Brāhmaṇa, ed. B.R. Sharma, Kendriya Sanskrit Vidyapitha, Tirupati, 1964.

Pañcaviṁśa Brāhmaṇa, English tr. W. Caland, Asiatic Society, Calcutta, 1931.

Kātyāyana Śrauta Sūtra, Chowkhamba Sanskrit Series Office, Banaras, 1939.

Lāṭyāyana Śrauta Sūtra, Munshiram Manoharlal, New Delhi, 1982.

Jātaka, English tr. E.B. Cowell, Motilal Banarsidass, Delhi, 1973.

Rāmāyaṇa, Geeta Press, Gorakhpur, 2024 Vikrami.

Mahābhārata, Geeta Press, Gorakhpur, 2024 Vikrami.

———, BORI, Poona, 1933-68.

Manusmṛti, ed. Rajvira Shastri, Arsh Sahitya Prachara Trust, Delhi, 1985.

———, ed. and tr. G. Buehler, Motilal Banarsidass, Varanasi, 1975.

Yājñavalkya Smṛti, ed. U. Pandey, Chowkhamba, Varanasi, 1967.

Viṣṇu Smṛti, English tr. Julius Jolly, Motilal Banarsidass, Delhi, 1965.

Yuga Purāṇa, JUPHS, vol. 20.

Thirukkural, English tr. A. Chakravorti, Madras, 1913.

Suśruta Saṁhitā, ed. Ambikadatta Shastri, Chowkhamba, Varanasi, 1959.

Arthaśāstra, ed. and tr. R.P. Kangle, University of Bombay, Bombay, 1965-72.

Kāmandakīya Nītisāra, English tr. M.L. Dutt, Chowkhamba Sanskrit Series, Varanasi, 1979.

———, ed. R.L. Mitra, Calcutta, 1972.

Amarakośa, ed. Hargovind Sastri, Chowkhamba Sanskrit Series, Varanasi, 1970.

Bṛhatsaṁhitā, ed. and tr. A. Jha, Chowkhamba Vidya Bhavan, Varanasi, 1969.

Raghuvaṁśa, ed. and tr. S. Chaturvedi, Bharat Prakashan Mandir, Aligarh, 2019 Vikrami.

Mālavikāgnimitram, ed. and tr. S. Chaturvedi, Bharat Prakashan Mandir, Aligarh, 2019 Vikrami.

Harṣacarita, ed. N.S. Press, Bombay, 1834 Śaka.

———, English tr. E.B. Cowell and F.W. Thomas, Motilal Banarsidass, Delhi, 1968.

Kādambarī, English tr. C.M Ridding, Oriental Book Reprint Corporation, New Delhi, 1974.

Matsya Purāṇa, ed. J.D. Akhtar, Delhi, 1972.

Agni Purāṇa (tr.), ed. J.L. Sastri, Motilal Banarsidass, Delhi, 1984.

Brahma Purāṇa (tr.), ed. J.L. Sastri, Motilal Banarsidass, Delhi, 1985.

Brahmāṇḍa Purāṇa (tr.), ed. J.L. Sastri, Motilal Banarsidass, Delhi, 1984.

Bhāgavata Purāṇa (tr.), ed. J.L. Sastri, Motilal Banarsidass, Delhi, 1987.

Mānasollāsa, ed. G.K. Shringodekar, Oriental Institute, Baroda, 1967.

Śiśupālavadha, ed. and tr. Hargovind Sastri, Chowkhamba Vidya Bhavan, Varanasi, 1955.

Naiṣadhīya Caritam, ed. N.R. Acharya, N.S. Press, Bombay, 1962.

Śukranītisāra, tr. B.K. Sarkar, Oriental Book Reprint Corporation, New Delhi, 1975.

SOME OTHER WORKS

Altekar, A.S., *The Coinage of the Gupta Empire and its Imitation*, Numismatic Society of India, Varanasi, 1957.

———, *Catalogue of the Gupta Gold Coins in the Bayana Hoard*, Numismatic Society of India, Bombay, 1954.

Gardner, Percy, *The Coins of Greek and Scythian Kings of Bactria and India in the British Museum*, Sagar Publications, New Delhi, 1971.

Lahiri, A.N., *Corpus of Indo-Greek Coins*, Poddar Publication, Calcutta, 1965.

Marshall, J., *Taxilā*, University Press, Cambridge, London, 1951.

———, *Mohenjo-daro and the Indus Civilization*, Indological Book House, Delhi, 1973.

M'Crindle, J.W., *Ancient India as Described by Megasthenese and Arrian*, Today and Tomorrow's Printers and Publishers, New Delhi, 1972.

———, *The Invasion of India by Alexander the Great*, Today and Tomorrow's Printers and Publishers, New Delhi, 1974.

Sachau, E., *Alberuni's India*, Indialog Publications Pvt. Ltd., Delhi, 2003.

Whitehead, R.B., *Catalogue of Coins in the Punjab Museum*, Lahore, vol. I, Oxford, 1914.

SECONDARY SOURCES

Agrawala, V.S., *Harṣacarita Eka Sāṁskṛtika Adhyayana*, Bihar Rashtrabhasha Parishad, Patna, 1953.

———, *India as Known to Pāṇini*, University of Lucknow, Lucknow, 1953.

Bachhofer, L., *Early Indian Sculpture*, Paris, 1929.

Banerjee, N.R., *The Iron Age in India*, Munshiram Manoharlal, New Delhi, 1965.

Barua, B.M., *Bhārhut*, Indological Book Corporation, Patna, 1979.

Barua, D.K., *An Analytical Study of Four Nikāyas*, Rabindra Bharati University, Calcutta, 1971.

Basham, A.L., *The Wonder That Was India*, Sidgwick and Jackson, London, 1954.

Basu, J., *India of the Age of Brāhmaṇas*, Sanskrit Pustak Bhandar, Calcutta, 1969.

Bongrad-Levin, G.M., *Studies in Ancient India and Central Asia*, Indian Studies, Calcutta, 1971.

Brij Bhushan, J., *The Costume and Textiles of India*, Taraporevala, Bombay, 1958.

Boucher, Francois, *A History of the Costume in the West*, Thames and Hudson, USA, 1987.

Bridget and Raymond Allchin, *The Rise of Civilization in India and Pakistan*, Cambridge University Press, Cambridge, 1996.

Chakravarty, P.C., *Art of War in Ancient India*, University of Dacca, Dacca, 1941.

Chakravorti, Ranabir, *Warfare for Wealth*, Firma KLM Pvt. Ltd., Calcutta, 1986.

Chakravarti, Swati, *Socio-Religious and Cultural Study of the Ancient Indian Coins*, B.R. Publishing Corporation, New Delhi, 1986.

Chaniotis, A. and Ducrey P. (eds.), *Army and Power in the Ancient World*, Franz Steiner Verlag, Stuttgart, 2002.

Chattopadhyaya, B., *The Age of the Kuṣāṇas: A Numismatic Study*, Punthi Pustak, Calcutta, 1967.

Chattopadhyaya, D., *History of Science and Technology in Ancient India: The Beginnings*, Firma KLM Pvt. Ltd., Calcutta, 1986.

Coomaraswamy, A.K., *History of Indian and Indonesian Art*, Munshiram Manoharlal, New Delhi, 1972.

Cunningham, A., *The Stūpa of Bhārhut*, Indological Book House, Varanasi, 1962.

———, *The Bhilsā Topes*, Indological Book House, Varanasi, 1966.

Dar, S.N., *Costumes of India and Pakistan*, Taraporevala, Bombay, 1958.

Das, A.C., *Ṛgvedic Culture*, Bharatiya Publishing House, Delhi, 1979.

Date, G.T., *The Art of War in Ancient India*, Calcutta, 1943.

Deekshit, V.R.R., *War in Ancient India*, Motilal Banarsidass, Delhi, 1987.

Dey, S.N., *Indian Life in Śukla Yajurveda*, Firma KLM Pvt. Ltd., Calcutta, 1985.

Dhavalikar, M.K., *Ajantā: A Cultural Study*, Deccan College, Poona, 1965.

Egerton, W., *Indian and Oriental Armour*, London, 1896.

Elkazi, Roshan, *Ancient Indian Costume*, Art Heritage, New Delhi, 1983.

Fergusson, J., *Tree and Serpent Worship*, Indological Book House, Delhi, 1971.

Foucher, A., *L'Art Greco Bouddhique Du Gandhāra*, vols. 1 & 2, Imprimerie National Paris, Paris, 1914, 1918.

Ghurye, G.S., *Indian Costume*, Popular Prakashan, Bombay, 1966.

Gode, P.K., *Studies in Indian Cultural History*, vol. 1, Vishveshvaranand Vedic Research Institute, Hoshiarpur, 1961; vol. 2, P.K. Gode Collected Works Publications Committee, Poona, 1960.

Gordon, D.H., *The Pre-historic Background of Indian Culture*, Bhulabhai Memorial Institute, Bombay, 1958.

Griffiths, J., *The Paintings in the Buddhist Cave Temples of Ajantā*, Secretary of State for India in Council, London, 1896.

Gupta, D.K., *Society and Culture in the Time of Daṇḍin*, Meharchand Lachhmandass, Delhi, 1972.

Habib, Irfan, *The Indus Civilization*, Tulika Books, New Delhi, 2002.

Hallade, M., *The Gandhāra Style and the Evolution of Buddhist Art*, Thames and Hudson, London, 1968.

Hazra, R.C., *Studies in Upapuraṇas*, 2 vols., Sanskrit College, Calcutta, 1958, 1963.

Hopkins, E.W., *The Social and Military Position of the Ruling Caste in Ancient India*, Bharat Bharati, Varanasi, 1972.

Ingholt, H.. *Gandhāran Art in Pakistan*, Lyons Islay, New York, 1957.

Joshi, N.P., *Life in Ancient Uttarāpatha*, Benaras, 1967.

Kak, R.C., *Ancient Monuments of Kashmir*, The Indian Society, London, 1933.

Kanaksabhai, V., *The Tamils Eighteen Hundred Years Ago*, Asian Educational Services, New Delhi, 1979.

Kane, P.V., *History of Dharmaśāstra* (5 vols.), BORI, Poona, 1941.

Lal, B.B., *The Earliest Civilization of South Asia*, Aryan Book International, New Delhi, 1997.

Law, B.C., *Indological Studies*, vol. I, Umesh Mishra Commemoration Committee, Allahabad, 1956.

Longhurst, A., *The Buddhist Antiquities of Nāgārjunikoṇḍa*, Madras Presidency, MASI, No. 54, 1938.

Macdonell, A.A. and A.B. Keith, *Vedic Index of Names and Subjects*, Motilal Banarsidass, Varanasi, 1958.

Mackay, E.J.H., *Further Excavations at Mohenjo-daro*, Indological Book Corporation, New Delhi, 1976.

———, *Early Indus Civilization*, Indological Book Corporation, Delhi, 1976.

Mahapatra, R.P., *Fashion Styles of Ancient India*, B.R. Publishing Corporation, Delhi, 1992.

Maisey, F.C., *Sāñchī and its Remains*, Indological Book House, Delhi, 1972.

Majumdar, R.C. (ed.), *The Vedic Age*, Bharatiya Vidya Bhavan, Bombay, 1965.

———, *The Age of Imperial Unity*, Bharatiya Vidya Bhavan, Bombay, 1960.

———, *The Classical Age*, Bharatiya Vidya Bhavan, Bombay, 1962.

Mani, B.R., *The Kuṣāṇa Civilization*, B.R. Publishing Corporation, Delhi, 1987.

Marshall, J., *A Guide to Sāñchī*, Manager of Publication, Delhi, 1936.

———, *Mohenjo-daro and the Indus Civilization*, Indological Book House, Delhi, 1973.

Marshall, J. and A. Foucher, *The Monuments of Sāñchī*, Archaeological Survey of India, Calcutta.

M'Crindle, J.W., *Ancient India as Described by Megasthenese and Arrian*, Today and Tomorrow's Printers and Publishers, New Delhi, 1972.

———, *The Invasion of India by Alexander the Great*, Today and Tomorrow's Printers and Publishers, New Delhi, 1974.

Mehta, R.N., *Pre-Buddhist India*, University of Bombay, Bombay, 1939.

Moti Chandra, *Prāchīna Bhāratīya Veśa-Bhūṣā*, Bharat Bhandar, Prayag, 2007 Vikramī.

Mukerjee, Sandhya, *Some Aspects of Social Life in Ancient India*, Narayana Publishing House, Allahabad, 1976.

Oppert, Gustava, *On the Weapons, Army Organization and Political Maxims of the Ancient Hindus*, New Order Books, Ahmedabad, 1967.

Pandey, G.C., *Dimensions of Ancient Indian Social History*, vol. II, Books and Books, Delhi, 1985.

Pant, G.N., *Studies in Indian Weapons and Warfare*, Army Educational Store, New Delhi, 1970.

———, *Indian Archery*, Agam Kala Prakashan, Delhi, 1978.

———, *Indian Arms and Armour*, Army Educational Store, Delhi, 1983.

Payne, Blanche, *History of Costume*, Harper and Row Publishers, New York.

Priyavrata, Vedavacaspati, *Prācīna Bhārata Meṅ Pratirakṣā Vyavasthā*, Meenakshi Prakashan, Meerut, 1984.

Ram Gopal, *India in Vedic Kalpasūtras*, Delhi, 1959.

Rapson, E.J., *Cambridge History of India*, vol. 1, S. Chand and Co., Delhi, 1955.

Rawson, P.S., *The Indian Sword*, Herbert Jenkins, Copenhagen, 1968.

Raychaudhuri, H.C., *Political History of Ancient India*, University of Calcutta, Calcutta, 1953.

Rice, T.T., *The Scythians*, Thames and Hudson, London, 1957.

Robinson, H. Russel, *Oriental Armour*, London, 1967.

Rosenfield, J.M., *The Dynastic Art of the Kushāṇs*, University of California Press, Berkeley, 1967.

Sharma, G.R., *Excavations at Kauśāmbī*, Allahabad University, Allahabad, 1960.

———, *Reh Inscription of Menander and the Indo-Greek Invasion of Gaṅgā Valley*, Avinash Prakashan, Allahabad, 1980.

Sharma, R.N., *Culture and Civilization as Revealed in Śrautasūtras*, Nag Publishers, Delhi, 1977.

Sharma R.S., *New Light on Ancient Indian Society and Economy*, Manaktalas, Bombay, 1966.

Shastri, A.M., *India as Seen in The Bṛhatsaṁhitā of Varāhamihira*, Motilal Banarsidass, Delhi, 1969.

Shastri, K.A. Nilakanta, *History of South India*, Oxford University Press, London, 1966.

Singh, Sabhapati, *Prācīna Bhārat meṅ Sainya Vyavasthā*, Durga Publications, Delhi, 1990.

Singh, S.D., *Ancient Indian Warfare with Special Reference to Vedic Period*, E.J. Brill, Lieden, 1965.

Smith, V.A., *The Jain Stūpa and Other Antiquities of Mathurā*, Indological Book Home, Delhi, 1969.

Srivastava, A.L., *Life in Sāñcī Sculptures*, Abhinava Publications, New Delhi, 1983.

Subrahmanian, N., *Saṅgam Polity*, Asia Publishing House, New Delhi, 1966.

Sulimirski, T., *The Sarmatians*, Thames and Hudson, London, 1970.

Thapar, Romila, *Ancient Indian Social History*, Orient Longman Limited, New Delhi, 1978.

———, *The Penguin History of Early India*, Penguin Books, London, 2002.

Thapliyal, U.P., *Foreign Elements in Ancient Indian Society*, Munshiram Manoharlal Publishers Pvt. Ltd., New Delhi, 1979.

———, *The Dhvaja*, B.R. Publishing Corporation, Delhi, 1983.

———, *Military Costumes of India*, Ministry of Defence, Delhi, 1991.

———, *Historical Perspectives of Warfare in india: Some Morale and Material Determinants* (ed. S.N. Prasad), Centre for Studies in Civilization, New Delhi, 2002

———, *Warfare in Ancient India: Organizational and Operational Dimensions*, Manohar, New Delhi, 2010.

Tripathi, R.S., *History of Ancient India*, Motilal Banarsidass, Delhi, 1981.

Vaidya, C.V., *Epic India*, vol. 1, Cosmo Publications, Delhi, 1984.

Vats, M.S., *Excavations of Harappa*, Manager of Publication, Delhi, 1984.

Watters, T., *On Yuan Chwang's Travels in India*, Munshiram Manoharlal Publishers Pvt. Ltd., Delhi, 1973.

Woodcock, G., *The Greeks in India*, Faber and Faber, London, 1966.

Yazdani, G., *Ajantā*, Oxford University Press, London, 1930.

Index

Ābharaṇa, 66
Ācchādana, 68, 142
Accoutrements, 56
Achaemenid invasions, 21
Adhivāsa, 53
Adhovāsa, 33, 43, 92
Ajina, 35
Akṣauhiṇī, 68
Alexander's invasion, 21-2
Ambara, 68, 69, 70, 81, 110
Aṁśupaṭṭa, 37
Aṅgad, 68
Aṅgulitrāṇa, 68, 73, 74
Añji, 57, 58
Aṅkuśa, 79, 145
Antarīya, 69
Anukarṣa, 68
Archer, 92; mounted, 126, 127, 128
Ardhoruka, 139
Ariṣṭa, 37
Armour, 50, 53, 71, 78, 95, 115, 122, 142, 147
Arrow, 49, 55, 56, 75, 95, 99, 124, 125
Āryan civilization, 18; tribes, 18
Asi, 56, 76, 97-8
Astara, 79
Āstaraṇa, 79
Asuras, 18
Aśvamedha, 18, 23, 25, 26, 27, 28, 29
Aurṇa, 34, 35
Avika, 35
Āyudha, 66
Āyudhāgārādhyakṣa, 94

Barks, 35; fibres, 40
Beard, 70, 71, 117
Bhāṇḍa, 68, 79, 81
Bhārhut soldier, 117, 119
Bilva, 37
Bit, 92, 107; curved, 127, 129, 146
Boots, 119, 121, 122, 128, 133, 141, 142
Bow, 49, 52, 55, 56, 99, 101; foreign types 123; composite, 124, 143
Brace, 55
Bracelets, 134

Camara, 66, 67, 80, 95, 109
Candana, 43
Caṇḍātaka, 139
Cāpa, 66
Caps, 44
Carma, 35, 66, 69, 74, 95, 96-7
Carmakavaca, 80
Chariot, 17, 21, 52, 128, 147; components, 59, 76, 77-8, 93, 103-5; horse, 60; upholstering, 77, 105; decline, 128
Chatra, 66
Cīnacolaka, 138
Cīnānśuka, 36
Cīnapaṭṭa, 36
Cīnasī, 36
Climatic factor, 32
Cloak, 119
Coat, 32, 43, 44, 53, 117, 122, 128, 138, 149
Coiffeur, 103
Corselets, 55
Costume, 41-2, 90, 101-2, 116-17

Cotton, 34, 35, 36, 38, 40, 90, 91
Cross-belts, 120

Deer-skin, 54
Dhotī, 42, 66, 70, 101, 119, 120, 134, 139, 149
Dhvaja, 58, 66, 70, 78, 79
Drāpi, 53
Dress material, 33, 35
Dukūla, 35, 40
Dyeing and cleaning, 36-7; *Vinaya* texts, 37; *Mahābhārata*, 37; *Arthaśāstra*, 37

Ear ornaments, 134
Elephant, 78, 79, 105; equipment, 79, 93, 105-6
Epic wars, 19
Epic soldier, 65-6
Equipment, 92

Falaka, 35
Flax, 40
Fillet, 48, 50, 119, 121
Foot-wear, 57, 74, 91, 103, 141
Foreign invasions, 21-2, 24-5; influence on costume, 43, 114

Gandhāra art, 115
Ghaṇṭā, 68
Girdle, 119
Gloves of skin, 66
Goad, 93, 105, 145
Graiveya, 68
Gupta conquests, 26-7

Hair, 70, 71, 103, 134
Hair-band, 36, 136, 149
Harappan age, 47-8; costume, 48-50; weapons and accoutrements, 49-50; standard, 50
Hastaghna, 57
Hastavāpa, 68, 73, 74
Helmet, 44, 55, 117, 123, 128, 136, 138, 149
Hemp, 40
Hides, 36
Horse, 43, 80; equipment of, 80-1, 92-3, 106-7, 127-8, 145-6; armour, 127-8

Indo-Greeks, 24-5
Iṣu, 56
Iṣudhi, 56, 75
Iron weapons, 19
Indus valley civilization, 17, 19, 35, 47-50; dress material, 34

Jackets, 41
Jātuṣa, 37
Javelin, 126
Jerkin, 134
Jyā, 56, 74

Kacagrahas, 67
Kakṣya, 79, 80, 105, 109, 145
Kālaka, 37
Kalapa, 68, 75
Kaṁbala, 79
Kampanas, 67
Kañcuka, 70, 96, 119, 134, 138
Kaṅkaṭa, 95
Kaṅṭhatrāṇa, 73, 96
Kaṇva rule, 23
Kārdaraṅga, 36
Kārpāsa, 34, 35, 138, 149
Kārpāsika, 35
Kaśā, 68, 80, 81
Kaṭibandha, 101, 120
Kauśeya, 34, 35
Kavaca, 40, 54, 66, 68, 70, 71, 72, 73, 80, 95-6
Kavāṭa, 96
Keyūra, 68
Khaḍga, 66, 67

Khādi, 57, 58
Khalina, 80, 81, 107, 145
Kilt, 119, 120
Kīṭaja, 35
Kṣauma, 34, 35, 40
Kūbara, 67
Kuṇḍala, 67, 69
Kūrpāsa, 96, 138
Kuśa, 34, 35
Kusāṇa, conquests, 25; empire 114; costume, 115
Kuthā, 79
Kuṭṭikṛta, 35

Lakṣa, 37
Leg-guard, 57
Linen, 34
Loin cloth, 50
Lohapaṭṭa, 122
Lohajālikā, 122
Lohitaka, 37

Magadha empire, 20
Mahābhārata, dress material in, 35
Mahājanapada age, 20
Maṇḍūra, 145, 146
Mañjiṣṭha, 37
Mauryan, army, 93-4; conquests, 22-3
Mausala, 75
Military costume, need for 32; Greek impact, 42-3; Śaka-Kuṣāṇa impact, 42-4
Military tactics, 42-3
Military vehicles, 59
Mohenjo-daro, cotton fabrics, 34; use of wool, 34
Mṛgājina, 35

Nāga rule, 25
Nāgodarika, 96
Nīla, 37
Niṣaṅga, 56, 75
Niṣka, 57, 58, 68

Nīvi, 53

Ox-cart, 17

Pakṣacarman, 145
Pantaloons, 115, 117
Paraśu, 56
Paricchada, 68
Parṇadhi, 56
Paruṣṇi, battle of, 18
Paṭsaṅgiṇī, 57
Paṭṭa, 95
Paṭṭaja, 35
Paṭṭikam, 69
Phāla, 35
Piṅgā, 139
Pīṭhaka, 80
Pratoḍa, 78
Pratyañcā, 69

Quiver, 52, 75, 99, 106, 146

Rāga, 36
Rājasūya, 18, 19, 35
Rāṅkava, 35, 79
Raṅku, 40
Raśmi, 60, 81
Raśnā, 60
Rathakāra, 59
Rein, 60, 93, 104, 107
Rocana, 37
Roman gladius, 126
Rukma, 57, 126

Saddle, 43, 60, 109, 127, 129, 145, 146
Śaka conquests, 24-5; influence, 43
Sakaccha, 42
Śakti, 56
Śalya, 56
Saṁjñā, 69
Saṁ-nahana, 77
Sāmuli, 36

Samūra, 36
Sandals, 91, 141
Saṇa, 34
Saṅgrāmasajjā, 65, 81
Sāṇi, 35
Śaṅkha, 69, 70
Śataghni, 67
Sātavāhana-Śaka conflict, 24
Śatulā, 139
Scabbard, 94, 125
Sewing, 40, 41
Sewn garment, 41
Shaving, 71
Sheath, 49
Shield, 97, 126, 136, 144
Shoes, 91, 103
Silk, 35, 36, 40
Śilpin, 72
Siṁhacarma, 35
Śipra, 55, 60
Śiprin, 60
Śirastrāṇa, 68, 70, 73, 96
Śirovastra, 101
Śiroveṣṭana, 110, 134
Sixteen *mahājanapadas*, 20
Skandhāvāra, 69
Skin garments, 34, 35, 53, 54
Sling, 49
Social bindings, 43
South Indian wars, 28-9
Spindle whorls, 38
Spinning and weaving, 37; at Mohenjo-daro, 37-8; in *Ṛgveda*, 38; in *Arthaśāstra*, 40
Sṛja, 57, 58
Sṛṇi, 145
Standard, 50, 94
Stavaraka, 36
Stirrup, 43, 109, 115, 127, 129, 145, 146
Sūcī, 41
Śuṅga rule, 23
Sutrādhyakṣa, 40, 95
Svasthāna, 139
Sword, 97-8, 125, 143-4
Syūta, 53

Talatra, 73
Talatrāṇa, 74
Tantuvāya, 40
Tanucchada, 68, 72, 73
Tanutra, 79
Tanutrāṇa, 68, 73
Tārpya, 53
Tilaka, 43
Tottra, 79, 145
Trousers, 33, 41, 43, 44, 120, 121, 122, 128, 133, 136
Tūṇa, 75, 79
Tunic, 110, 115, 117, 119, 120, 133, 136
Tūṇīra, 69, 81
Turban, 48, 134, 136

Uddīcyaveśa, 122, 141
Upānaha, 57, 103
Upāsaṅga, 68, 75
Upaskara, 68
Uracchada, 68
Urapaṭṭa, 59
Uṣṇīṣa, 33, 43, 68, 69, 73, 81, 92
Uttarīya, 33, 38, 42, 43, 48, 66, 69, 81, 92, 101, 149

Vaijayanta, 79, 106
Vainuka, 145
Vājapeya, 18
Vajra, 56
Vākāṭaka conquests, 27
Vāla, 35
Valkala, 35
Vārabāṇa, 96, 138
Vardhanas, 28
Varma, 40, 53, 54, 55, 66, 68, 69, 70, 71, 72, 95
Varūtha, 57
Vāsa, 53
Vasana, 53, 69, 81, 110
Vāsas, 53, 59
Vāsī, 57-8
Vastra, 53, 66, 68, 69, 81, 101, 110
Vāyaka, 40

Vaturiṇā padā, 57
Vedic civilization, 17, 18
Vehicles of war, 76, 103-7, 144
Vimāna, 78, 79
Vrātya costume, 58-9
Vyāghracarma, 35
Vyajana, 66

Waist-band, 101-2, 120, 141
Weapons, 17, 19, 49, 50, 52, 55-6, 66, 74-6, 92, 93, 115, 134, 142-4
Whip, 60
Wool, 34, 35, 38, 40
Woollens, 36

Yavana influence, 119, 120
Yoktra, 77, 107